101 THINGS

YOU DIDN'T KNOW ABOUT

EINSTEIN

101 THINGS
YOU DIDN'T KNOW ABOUT
EINSTEIN
SEX, SCIENCE, AND THE
SECRETS OF THE UNIVERSE

Cynthia Phillips, Ph.D. & Shana Priwer

BARNES & NOBLE

NEW YORK

To our children, *Zoecyn, Elijah,* and *Benjamin*

This 2007 edition published by Barnes & Noble, Inc.,
by arrangement with Adams Media, an F+W Publications Company.

ISBN-13: 978-0-7607-9272-8
ISBN-10: 0-7607-9272-0

Printed and bound in the United States of America

10 9 8 7 6 5 4 3 2 1

CONTENTS

Part 1. | Einstein's Personal Background and Family Life 1

Part 4. | War, Religion, and Politics........ 159

Part 5. Awards, Achievements, and
Other Intellectual Pursuits 189

INTRODUCTION

History is debatable, especially when it comes to its views on individuals. As the years roll on and perception and popular opinion change, so too does history's view of events and achievements. Even with many of the figures and events of the last century, there is already a great deal of conjecture as to the how and the why of their lives and the depth of their impact. JFK, Gandhi, Henry Ford—all these people have had tremendous impact on the last 100 years, but details of their lives have begun to shade modern opinion.

Of all the influential figures of the twentieth century who stand out in our minds, few have had such profound and lasting influence as Albert Einstein. What makes Einstein different from other iconic figures of modern history is that, while many people know the importance of his scientific work, most people have little idea exactly what that work is or how greatly it affects the world today.

While just about everyone knows Einstein is responsible for the theory of relativity, how many people know that Einstein worked on a safer type of refrigerator or developed hearing aids? Or that he made a few scientific blunders and one of his students actually spotted a mistake in one of his papers? Then there's his personal life. Was Einstein a womanizer? Well, for one thing, he left his first wife after having an affair with his long-lost distant cousin.

Beyond his vast impact on the world of science, Einstein was also active politically and socially. He parlayed his fame into influence that he used as often and as wisely as he could. After fleeing Germany as the Nazi regime grew, he helped international humanitarian organizations provide aid to refugees less fortunate than he. He lent support to the fledging nation of Israel, a nation where he was so well respected that they offered him a position within the government.

Einstein did not stop there. A devoted pacifist, he struggled for the later part of his life to influence various world governments to find a way to solve international disputes without resorting to violence and war. Yet at one point in his life, Einstein joined with some of his contemporaries and drafted a letter to the president of the United States suggesting that possession of a nuclear weapon might make an effective deterrent to war.

It is obvious that Einstein was a complex and accomplished man. So much so that he has become the modern embodiment of what we think of as a genius. *101 Things You Didn't Know about Einstein* will help you see into all aspects of Albert's life: personal, professional, religious, and social. These insights will help you understand one of the most important figures in all of history, not just the past 100 years of it.

Part 1

Einstein's Personal Background and Family Life

Thanks to television, magazines, and the Internet, we're used to knowing a tremendous amount of information about politicians and celebrities. Perhaps we have a little too much immediate knowledge. That wasn't the case for much of Einstein's life. Certainly he achieved a level of recognition almost unheard of for a scientist, but it does not translate to a tremendous knowledge of the man's personal life.

It is ironic that many figures in history who are considered self-made are often those most deeply affected by their upbringing and the world around them. Einstein was no different. His family shaped much of how Einstein would see the world, and conversely, his children became a reflection of how that worldview had changed throughout his lifetime, as research and years of striving for greatness shaped his opinions.

In these first chapters, we'll get to see how Einstein's personal relationships impacted all aspects of his life including his reputation as a womanizer, his role as a father, and even some of his lesser known habits and hobbies.

1. Einstein's parents and extended family: genealogy of the genius

Albert Einstein was born in Ulm, Germany, on March 14, 1879, the first child of Hermann and Pauline Einstein, a middle-class German-Jewish couple. In 1880, Hermann and Pauline moved their small family to Munich, where Einstein's sister, Maria, was born a year later.

Einstein's family clearly played a large role in encouraging his curiosity and natural gifts. His immediate and extended families were reasonably well off and were able to provide him with books and other objects that allowed him to advance his studies.

Both intelligence and aptitude for science ran in Einstein's family. Einstein's mother was a homemaker and a musician. His uncle Jakob ran an engineering company, Einstein & Cie. Hermann, his father, was an electrician as well as an amateur electrical inventor. He actually established an electrotechnical factory in Munich soon after Albert was born, along with his brother Jakob, but Hermann didn't have the best luck with business ventures.

While his father's income came and went, Einstein's grandparents and other relatives were able to help out enough that he never had to suffer. The financial stability that Einstein's family provided is significant in that Einstein had the luxury of being able to focus on intellectual pursuits as a child, rather than having to fight for mere survival.

Einstein's family was also emotionally supportive. Hermann and Pauline provided a stimulating environment, one in which Einstein thrived.

Both his parents were educated, and they, in turn, valued their children's education. By the time he was eleven years old, Einstein was reading philosophy and religion, in addition to his regular school courses. His uncle Jakob instilled a love of mathematics in young Einstein, and his uncle Caesar Koch inspired him to study science. Above all, Einstein was a curious child. He asked questions and sought answers. He was patient and determined, sticking with a problem until his curiosity was satisfied.

His parent's marriage was a happy one, and marital discontent doesn't appear to have been a distraction for Einstein either. Lack of major life issues probably gave Einstein much more freedom to develop intellectually than he might have had under different circumstances.

The religious atmosphere in the Einstein home also contributed to the ways in which he would come to formulate his theories later in life. His parents were nonobservant Jews, meaning they were Jewish but did not observe all the rituals and ceremonies of the religion. They did not keep a kosher household, nor did they attend synagogue services regularly. They did, however, respect Judaism, and they instilled that same respect for religion in their children. In part, perhaps, this religious atmosphere laid the foundation for some of Einstein's later struggles. As a child, he was already starting to think about the dichotomy between science and religion, and creationism versus evolution.

When Hermann's business in Germany failed in 1890, he was offered the chance to set up a factory in Pavia (a town near Milan, Italy). At this point, the rest of his family moved to Italy, but Einstein initially remained behind in Germany to finish his schooling for several more years.

Since the family house had been sold, Einstein moved in with relatives for the duration of his stay in Germany, but he was apparently unhappy about his prospects there. He left Munich in 1894 without finishing his degree and moved to Milan with his family. In 1895, after failing the entrance exams for the Eidgenössische Technische Hochschule (ETH), in Switzerland, Einstein spent a year studying in Aarau before successfully enrolling in the ETH in 1896.

Hermann died in 1902. Einstein would later describe his father's passing as one of the greatest shocks in his life to date. At that point, he threw himself into his work, and this renewed energy probably contributed to his major works of 1905. After a bout with cancer, Einstein's mother, Pauline, died in 1920. Her death led Einstein to focus on his work even more, paving the way for major events in the near future.

2. MUSIC IN EINSTEIN'S EARLY YEARS

Music would play a large role throughout Einstein's life. Thanks to his mother, he began piano lessons at age six. She was herself an accomplished pianist and passed on a love of music to her children. Einstein would persist in both musical study and performance for years to come.

While continuing piano lessons throughout his childhood, Einstein also played the violin. He began private studies at age five, on the request of his mother who was trying to ameliorate his early problems in school.

Although he threw a tantrum (and a chair) at his first teacher, luckily he was able to persist and become an accomplished amateur musician. Not incredibly fond of the violin at first, he continued to play the stringed instrument throughout his life, and it became one of many things that made Einstein a unique individual. In his later years in Princeton, he was often seen carrying his violin case around town, and his favorite composers were said to be Mozart, Bach, and Handel. Scores by these composers were part of his personal library and were donated to the Jewish National & University Library in 1987 after the death of his stepdaughter Margot Einstein.

Music and mathematics share many common elements, and Einstein undoubtedly found the same love in both. While he played largely for relaxation and not explicitly for study, it is no coincidence that music remained an important part of Einstein's life. Often, he was said to solve complex mathematical problems in his head while improvising on the violin (which he nicknamed "Lina"), and taking refuge in music helped him resolve many scientific and personal dilemmas. Mathematics and music are inextricably linked. From the number of notes in an octave to the number of beats in a measure, math creates an order and definition for many aspects of musical theory and performance. It is therefore not surprising that orderly progressions of composers like Bach might stimulate Einstein's great mathematical mind.

Some contend, in fact, that Einstein would never have arrived upon the theory of relativity had it not been for his love of the violin. His intense desire to understand formula and theory transitioned from music to science. More than that, though, it's possible that using music as an outlet for his scientific exploration allowed Einstein to see science in an entirely new light. This advantage may have given him insight that could have come from no other source.

3. EINSTEIN'S SISTER MAJA EINSTEIN WINTELER

Einstein's sister, Maria (nicknamed Maja) was his closest friend as a child. Born in 1881, she was two years younger than Albert, and he was always protective of her. They explored the German countryside as children, often roaming around the lakes near Munich. She was his constant companion until he separated from his family in 1894; Maja and their parents moved to Italy for their father's business, while Albert remained behind to finish up his schooling in Munich.

Even after this first separation, the two always remained close; they were said to have understood each other completely. This sort of relationship was unique in Einstein's life, throughout which other people appeared to have come and gone. Maja was a constant. Of course, even the friendliest of siblings have their moments of rivalry; Einstein apparently once threw a bowling ball at her during a temper tantrum. Luckily, both appear to have survived the experience.

Maja eventually married Paul Winteler, son of the headmaster of the school Einstein had attended in Aarau. Einstein was also close to the

Winteler family, forming a close relationship with Paul and his sisters, Marie and Anna. (Anna would later go on to marry one of Einstein's best friends, Michele Besso.)

In 1939, Maja was living in Florence but Jews were rapidly becoming ostracized, due to Mussolini's rule. Upon relocating to the United States that year, Maja moved in with her brother at his home in Princeton, New Jersey. Her husband Paul moved to Geneva at this time, living with his sister Anna and her family. Maja continued to live with her brother until her death in 1951. Einstein was completely devoted to his sister, and he remained so until the end of her life. Unfortunately, Maja never saw her husband again after her move to America. Although the couple planned to reunite after the war, Maja suffered a stroke that left her unable to travel.

Maja produced a biography of her famous brother in 1924, and much of what is known about Einstein's childhood comes from her writings including much of what we know about Einstein's delay in speech.

4. EINSTEIN AND OTHER FAMOUS DYSLEXICS

The word "dyslexia" comes from the Greek and actually means "trouble with words." It is a language disability that interferes with reading, writing, and spelling, and it affects people from all professions and all walks of life. Sometimes, it affords them new ways of thinking and realizing their thoughts.

$\Sigma\theta\frac{\iota}{\pi\Delta}\lambda$ "$\frac{\alpha}{\pi\theta}$ "$\pi\theta_\Delta\Sigma\theta\frac{\iota}{\pi\Delta}\lambda$ "$\frac{\alpha}{\pi\theta}\frac{\sigma}{4\pi}\chi\overset{\alpha}{\Delta}\pi\Sigma\theta\frac{\alpha}{\pi\Delta}\lambda$ "$\frac{\alpha}{\pi\theta}\frac{\sigma}{4\pi}\chi\overset{\alpha}{\Delta}\pi\theta_\Delta$"

Dyslexia is categorized as a syndrome, unrelated to intelligence or potential.

There are a variety of stories and myths surrounding Einstein's alleged learning disability. True, he didn't learn to speak until he was well into his toddler years. His early trouble in school was sometimes attributed to mild dyslexia. However, others assert that Einstein wasn't disabled at all. The fact that he learned to speak later might have just meant that he was shy and kept to himself. He certainly tended toward introversion as an adult and might simply have been expressing this character trait from an early age. He was reading physics texts and difficult philosophy tracts in his pre-teen years, this again does not support the suggestion that he might have had a learning disability.

It is true that Einstein failed the entrance examinations for the Eidgenössische Technische Hochschule (ETH), in Switzerland, the first time he applied. One must take into account, though, that he first applied when he was sixteen years old—two years younger than usual. Also, it's possible that he just didn't study enough for the exams or wasn't good at taking that kind of exam; either scenario would have had no bearing on whether or not he had a learning disability. What it comes down to is that, since such diagnoses weren't often made in the late-nineteenth century, any thoughts on Einstein's disability are basically speculation.

However, if Einstein was in fact dyslexic, did this alleged learning disability prevent Einstein from conducting amazing research? Absolutely not. Did it keep him from achieving his goals? Not at all. However, even a slight language disorder might have influenced some aspects of Einstein's development in ways that would seep into his adult professional career.

For example, it's been said that Einstein always had difficulty in searching for words. Expressing himself verbally was never his strong point. This impediment might have rendered him shyer as a child, and perhaps was with him throughout his life. He did, however, conquer the issue when push came to shove. He learned to visualize his ideas first, and this creative approach to the problem helped provide a solution. When his activism demanded that he become a public speaker, Einstein ventured out to make speeches and voice his opinions. While he preferred a quiet life close to home, the activist path he chose for himself demanded that he become more of a public figure; he overcame the odds and did what he had to do.

Could mild dyslexia actually have helped Einstein achieve the amazing success that he did? It's certainly possible. It's said that some dyslexics have trouble focusing or concentrating, and often tend to daydream rather than focusing on a specific task. Daydreaming and mental exploration were precisely the kinds of thought patterns that allowed Einstein to arrive at his pronouncement of relativity. Many of Einstein's breakthroughs were in fact based on "thought-experiments." A more structured mind, for example, might never have been able to conceive of the world the way Einstein did. And what a shame that would have been.

Einstein was not the only scientist ever to face the challenge of dyslexia. Thomas Edison, Alexander Graham Bell, and Louis Pasteur all suffered from dyslexia.

5. Einstein's first wife Mileva Maric Einstein

The year 1898 marked the first time that Einstein succumbed to something other than science—love. "Bookish" is a term generally used to describe Mileva Maric (1875–1948). She was four years older than Einstein, walked with a limp, and was not known for her beauty. In spite of these things, Einstein was enchanted by his Hungarian classmate when he met her at the Eidgenössische Technische Hochschule (ETH).

To some extent, it was sheer fortune that allowed Einstein and Mileva to meet. While women were admitted into the ETH, they were still treated as second-class citizens in many regards—they were not even allowed to vote in Switzerland at that time. Had Einstein attended another school, or had the ETH been less liberal in its dealings with women, their union might never have happened. Even with this relatively new-found liberalism, Mileva was the only woman in her class at the ETH, so her meeting with Einstein was, to some extent, unavoidable. In fact, Mileva was the only female student in physics during Einstein's entire time at the ETH.

It seems natural that Einstein would fall in love with a scientist—someone with whom he could exchange intellectual ideas. More importantly, perhaps, Mileva was someone who understood Einstein because they shared the same interests, academically and otherwise. She was one of the brightest students at the ETH, considered by many to be a brilliant physicist. She kept pace with Einstein throughout their school years, taking most of the same courses he did.

Shortly after meeting, Einstein and Mileva moved in together. Legend has it that they shared everything, including class notes and textbooks. They were supposedly quite compatible in most aspects of life. Mileva took on some of the stereotypical female roles of a wife even from this early period: cooking, cleaning, laundry, paying bills, and even reminding Einstein to stop working and eat a meal.

Despite their compatibilities in other ways, the two came from different religious backgrounds. Mileva had been raised in the Eastern Orthodox Christian tradition, while Einstein had been raised in a Jewish household, although admittedly unobservant.

Einstein's parents, particularly his mother, were opposed to their union from the beginning. Perhaps Einstein's parents disliked Mileva because of her Serbian backgound. More likely, though, his mother felt threatened by this new woman. Mileva was modern and smart, and Einstein was clearly taken by her. His mother probably felt challenged, as if she were no longer the primary woman in her son's life.

Einstein tried to mollify his parents and rectify the situation by spending vacations with his mother and showing her his devotion. Although this tactic may have worked to some extent, it probably didn't help his relationship with Mileva. Einstein and Mileva often spent vacations apart because he would return home to his family, where Mileva was not welcome. This division in the family may have been cause for strife. Einstein tried to convince Mileva that she was, in fact, the most important woman in his life, but there isn't much evidence for how successful he was.

Although they faced such difficulties, Albert and Mileva were married in 1903. Einstein's mother continued to object strongly to their union, but the couple ultimately could not be deterred. No doubt, however, their marriage was a rocky one, and the couple ultimately divorced in 1919.

6. Einstein's daughter Liserl Einstein

Einstein and Mileva had their first child in January 1902. A daughter, Liserl, was born at the home of Mileva's parents in Serbia. While early twentieth century society was far more considerate to men who fathered children out of wedlock than to the women who bore them, Einstein likely did not want to jeopardize his career by making news of this child public.

While no one knows exactly what happened to Liserl, it is generally thought that she was put up for adoption, probably in Serbia, because of the damage that having had an illegitimate child could have done to both Mileva and Einstein's burgeoning careers. Very little is known about Liserl Einstein because she was born out of wedlock at a time when such children were subject to a lifetime of prejudice. While some think she lived to adulthood, most think she either died at birth or within a few years thereafter.

Some people think Liserl might have been either retarded or born with Down's syndrome, a chromosomal anomaly that occurs in about one out of every 1,000 births to women under thirty (Mileva would have been seventeen years old in 1902). A child can be born with Down's syndrome without the mother having the condition, so it's possible that Liserl was in fact born with it. It also might explain her abandonment, since turn-of-the-century attitudes toward the disabled were not as enlightened as they are today. However, there is not much positive evidence to support this theory.

Others believe that, based on letters from Einstein to his wife, the baby died as a young child from scarlet fever. Still others contend that, unable to put her up for adoption, Mileva left her with relatives in the Vojvodina region of Serbia. Clearly, the lack of verifiable information has caused much speculation. Author Michele Zackheim spent years researching what might have happened to Liserl and presented her findings in her 1999 book entitled *Einstein's Daughter: The Search for Liserl*. Authors have also written fictional novels involving Liserl, wondering about what her life might have been like. One example can be seen in *Mrs. Einstein*, a novel by Anna McGrail that posits an imaginary tale of what might have happened to Liserl.

7. Einstein's elder son Hans Albert Einstein

Albert and Mileva's first legitimate child was born in 1904. Hans Albert (1904–1973) lived an interesting life that followed partially in his father's footsteps. After completing his elementary school education in Zurich, Switzerland, Hans received a diploma in civil engineering from the Swiss

Federal Institute of Technology in Zurich in 1926. He then received a doctor of technical sciences degree from the same university in 1936. Between 1926 and 1930, Hans lived in Germany, working in the town of Dortmund as a steel designer. As a graduate student in Zurich, he was fascinated by the problem of transporting sediment via flowing water and wrote his doctoral dissertation on this issue. In fact, scientists and engineers worldwide still use his thesis to this day. Hans married Frieda Knecht in 1927. She was a German instructor at the University of Zurich. Hans and Frieda moved to the United States in 1938, several years after Albert Einstein moved there. Hans would continue his research into sediment transportation at the U.S. Agricultural Experiment Station in South Carolina until 1943. At that point, he moved to the U.S. Department of Agriculture Cooperative Laboratory, which was part of the California Institute of Technology. Hans remained a researcher there until 1947, when he became a faculty member at the University of California at Berkeley. Hired first as an associate professor, Hans later became a full professor of hydraulic engineering. Hans took on several roles while at the university—he was a teacher, a researcher, and also a practicing engineer. Well-known during his career, he received numerous awards and honors, including the Certificate of Merit given by the U.S. Department of Agriculture in 1971.

His first wife Frieda died in 1958. Shortly afterward, Hans married Elizabeth Roboz, who worked as a biochemist at the Stanford University Medical School. She later became a professor of neurology at the San Francisco Medical Center, part of the University of California.

Professional inclinations aside, Hans enjoyed the same sort of entertainment as his father. He was a big fan of music, as well as sailing and walking. Sailing on San Francisco Bay was one of his favorite pastimes. More social than his father, Hans was known for his willingness to spend time with his family and friends. Hans also spent much time with his graduate students and was known for his patience and devotion. Like his father, though, Hans also understood the importance of making professional connections in his field, and he made every effort to be in touch with current experts in the field of sediment transport.

Einstein and his older son had a good relationship. Both being scientists, they could relate to each other on multiple levels. Over the years and despite various separations, they seem to have gotten along well most of the time. They had a mutual respect for each other's intelligence and abilities. After suffering a heart attack in June 1973, Hans Albert Einstein died in July of that same year.

8. Einstein's younger son Eduard Einstein

Eduard was born in 1910. Unlike his older brother, Eduard did not excel in the sciences. He enjoyed reading the works of Shakespeare as a child, supposedly reading them on his own by the age of five. Eduard shared his father's abilities with music and showed early signs of genius, but he does not appear to have excelled particularly in any one area. Eduard was always considered the most sensitive member of the Einstein clan. He was reportedly close to his father until Albert and Mileva's separation in 1914.

He studied pre-med in college and was interested in becoming a psychologist. Unfortunately during this period, he suffered a mental breakdown that would later be determined to be either the onset of schizophrenia or a serious case of depression. Albert and Mileva didn't appear to have reconciled for their son's sake; their lack of communication may have furthered Eduard's feelings of alienation and desperation. Albert Einstein did return to Switzerland to be by his son's side, although he doesn't appear to have been of great use in resolving his son's crisis; he did not provide the daily visits or phone calls that could have helped Eduard in his recovery. Eduard was said to have worshipped Sigmund Freud, hanging Freud's picture over his bed and constantly praising his therapeutic methods.

Eduard's relationship with his father does not seem to have been very close. Einstein did not live with Eduard during his early and formative years (the period of time when Einstein and Mileva were separated, and later divorced), and Eduard spent far more time with his mother than he did with his father. In letters written to his father, Eduard actually indicated that he identified strongly with his mother on several levels. Both Eduard and Mileva felt Einstein had abandoned them, and they both were hesitant to recognize their own achievements and capabilities.

Einstein did try to encourage his younger son to find fulfillment rather than fame. In a letter from 1932 he is said to have told Eduard, "Don't fall victim to the devil of ambition and vanity . . . Not the desire for the achievement but love of the things themselves can lead to something worthwhile." While this advice was probably heartfelt, it may not have helped Eduard to gather his thoughts and focus on any specific area of interest. In addition it is possible that because the Einstein family was so successful in physics and science, Eduard may have felt undervalued or insignificant for having interests in other areas.

Eduard lived with his mother until her death in 1948, and then he was placed in a psychiatric institution. He died in an institution near Zurich in 1965.

9. What kind of father was Einstein?

As one of the great physicists and theorists of all time, Albert Einstein certainly led a busy life. But, as everyone knows, the day only has twenty-four hours and even the most famous scientists have to make room for personal affairs. Einstein had a family, which led to hard decisions with regard to the amount and quality of attention he was able to pay them.

Supposedly, although Einstein was not against the idea of being a father, he didn't understand children very well. Einstein thought it would be interesting to have a child and didn't have many options when Mileva became pregnant for the second time. While Einstein celebrated the birth of his second child, Hans, he was never completely overtaken by fatherly duties. Einstein was not a role model for stay-at-home dads, especially when his children were infants. He would often research, write, and discuss science with friends while he was supposed to be taking care of the children.

On the other hand, sometimes he would set his work aside for hours on end just to play with the children. It seems that Einstein was able to keep his personal and professional careers in an acceptable balance, at least during his early years as a father.

Einstein's experience of fatherhood was doubled in 1910 with the arrival of his second son, Eduard. His approach to parenting two children seems to have been similar to when Hans was his only child. Family was important and to be cherished, and love was in abundance, despite Einstein's obsession with his work. Einstein was reputed to have been able to work despite a baby's crying, or just about any other interruption.

In the earlier part of his life, when Einstein was still married to Mileva, married life treated him well. He was cared for, and in turn, he loved his children deeply. His children seem to have responded well to him, and they respected the work and research of which he was a part. Nevertheless, when Einstein moved to Berlin in 1914 and his wife and children, vacationing in Switzerland, were unable to join him, the separation must have been difficult for father and sons alike.

Despite his and Mileva's marital problems, Einstein wanted to be popular with his children, and he tried to keep things positive for them rather than exposing them to the troubles he and his wife were having. His efforts at protection, though, probably led to their feeling isolated and nervous, as if things were beyond their control. A modern approach to parenting would probably have had Einstein and family in counseling to help the children work through their feelings about their parent's divorce, but such therapy wasn't the norm in the early twentieth century.

By 1933, when Einstein moved to the United States with his second wife Elsa Lowenthal, Hans was twenty-nine years old and Eduard was twenty-three. Einstein's children, like most people's kids, were a source of both pride and dismay at various points throughout their lives. They followed their father's example of science and humanitarianism to varying degrees.

10. WHY EINSTEIN WORKED AT THE PATENT OFFICE

As a young man, Einstein initially thought he might be interested in a career in electrical engineering, like his father and uncle. After failing to get into Zurich's prestigious Eidgenössische Technische Hochschule (the ETH, also known as the Swiss Federal Polytechnic Institute), he attended an intermediary secondary school in Aarau, Switzerland, and earned his diploma in a year. He then reapplied to the ETH, was admitted in 1896 and graduated with degrees in physics and mathematics. While at the ETH, Einstein pursued his interest in laboratory science, but he didn't attend all his classes. As a result, he relied on friends for assistance with class notes, particularly before exams.

Marcel Grossmann, one of his good friends at the ETH, would come to play an important role in Einstein's life, and not just when it came to sharing class notes or studying for tests. Grossmann would later help Einstein with some of the mathematical theory behind relativity, and Grossmann's father even helped Einstein to get his first full-time job.

Einstein graduated from the ETH in 1900, albeit with the lowest grade point average in the class. It seems that after graduation, Einstein didn't exactly have an easy time falling into the right professional niche. An education from a prestigious university does not always equal a free ticket to a great job. Even Einstein had to start at the bottom and work his way up to a point where he was respected and trusted by scholars and the public alike.

Einstein actually applied to become a teacher at the ETH along with several of his classmates (including Marcel Grossmann), but he wasn't successful. Einstein did ultimately get a job teaching math and physics at the Technical High School in Winterthur, where he served as an Aushilfslehrer (assistant lecturer), but the work was only part-time. Part-time work didn't pay well enough, so he had to look for other work as well. He obtained a temporary teaching job at a school in Schaffhausen, and between these jobs and private tutoring sessions, Einstein was able to earn a living for the next year.

Eventually, Einstein moved to Bern, Switzerland, where he continued to look for other jobs but had a difficult time. His university professors knew he skipped many classes, and they refused to write him the recommendations he needed to get a job. Then, in 1902, Grossmann's father recommended him to the Swiss patent office, located in Bern, and he was hired as a technical expert, third class. Working as a civil servant may not have been the most exciting career choice, but it paid the bills and left Einstein with plenty of time to do his own research on the side. Einstein did well at this job, and four years later in 1906, he was promoted to technical expert, second class. He worked at the patent office from 1902 to 1909, and he actually did some of his most significant early research during these years.

In 1905, Einstein finally received his doctorate degree from the University of Zurich. His dissertation was called "A New Determination of Molecular Dimensions." The stage was set for what would come to be some of Einstein's most influential and revolutionary work: the writing of his three major papers in the period beginning in 1905.

The year 1905 is what some historians have called Einstein's *annus mirabilis,* his miracle year. The cliché of the Swiss patent clerk revolutionizing physics is true—while working in the patent office, Einstein published three papers that shook up the scientific community. The first of these three papers was on the photoelectric effect, and this work would eventually earn him the Nobel Prize.

Einstein had taken the job at the patent office because he needed to earn a living, and the job afforded him plenty of time for his own work. But it was still a day job with responsibilities that required his time and energy, and those responsibilities would eventually take a toll on his research.

When Einstein's main papers on relativity were presented, the outpouring of support was enormous. He was beginning to gain recognition as one of Europe's foremost scientific thinkers and researchers, and the idea of making a living as a scientist was becoming more and more real. In 1909, Einstein earned an associate professorship at the University of Zurich, and he was able to make a clean break with the patent office.

11. EINSTEIN'S REPUTATION AS A WOMANIZER

Einstein wasn't reputed to be the most faithful of husbands. He fathered a child, Liserl, out of wedlock in 1902, and went on to marry the child's mother. While married to Mileva Maric between 1903 and 1919, the couple appeared to have been very much in love; Albert wrote to Mileva, "How happy I am to have found in you an equal creature who is equally strong and independent as I am." Despite their mutual affection, Einstein's wandering eye appears to have gotten the better of him. While on a trip to Berlin in 1912, he met with his distant cousin Elsa and began an adulterous interlude. She took care of him when he became ill in 1917, and they went on to marry in 1919 soon after his divorce from Mileva became final.

He also was reputed to have had numerous affairs over the years of his marriage to Elsa. There were rumors that Einstein was attracted to not only Elsa but also her daughter Ilse; he was said to have married Elsa (the older) only after being rejected by Ilse (the younger, who was 22 at the time).

Einstein was prolific in both verbal and written discourse and seems to have applied a romantic touch to his prose, especially when writing members of the opposite gender. One biographer even described the attraction that many women felt to Einstein as magnetic. While married to Elsa, he developed a close friendship with Betty Neumann, the niece of a friend. A letter from Einstein to Ms. Neumann, in January 1924, expresses his feelings for her in a lightly flirtatious tone; "As I mustn't run after you, it is my everlasting hope to meet you accidentally . . . laugh at me, the old donkey, and find somebody who is 10 years younger than me, and who loves you just as much as I do." His second wife Elsa allowed Einstein to have regular visits with Betty Neumann, which may have been a reason that their marriage lasted until her death in 1936.

In his later years, Einstein had other relationships as well. He had a secretary named Helen Dukas, a Swabian woman from southwest Germany, who moved to the United States with him; she started work for Einstein in 1928 and continued the relationship until his death. In addition to secretarial duties, Dukas archived and collected Einstein's various works. She was a close personal friend of Einstein's and, some say, their relationship was more than simply professional; she cared for Einstein after the death of his wife Elsa.

Einstein's last encounter seems to have been with Johanna Fantova, a librarian at Princeton University, who later moved into his house on Mercer Street. The two actually met in Berlin in 1929, and Fantova moved to Princeton in 1939. Aside from their organizing his personal library together, the two appeared to have been quite close. They were constant companions during his last years, going on sailing adventures and attending concerts. Fantova kept all of Einstein's notes and poems, later compiling them into various collections.

12. Einstein's move to Berlin

In 1914, World War I broke out, heralding several important changes in Einstein's life. That year, he was invited by the famous scientist Max Planck to become director of the Kaiser Wilhelm Institute of Physics, a position he accepted and retained until 1933. Although Einstein became recognized as one of the most brilliant minds of his time, constantly proving oneself is an integral part of a successful career in research and academia; Einstein's moving to a prime academic institution was a large step in this direction. Kaiser Wilhelm provided Einstein with an opportunity to conduct his own science and research, under his own demands, schedules, and guidelines. At the time, this job was one of the best-paying positions that a physicist could have had.

In addition to the position at Kaiser Wilhelm, Einstein was also appointed a professor at the University of Berlin in 1914, furthering both his academic and research goals. Berlin was a good place to be, as the Prussian Academy of Science had many of the day's most famous scientists as members. These positions gave Einstein the recognition he needed to further his career. Also interesting is the fact that Einstein did not reapply for German citizenship on moving to Berlin in 1914; he was one of only a few German academics who did not support the war, and this aspect of his personal ethic became an integral part of his public persona.

While the war years were good to Einstein professionally, they took an enormous toll on his marriage to Mileva. The family moved to Berlin from Switzerland in April 1914, and that summer, Mileva and the children took a vacation in Switzerland. Separate vacations were not uncommon in the Einstein household. Albert usually went home to visit his family, and Mileva was generally not invited along for those excursions. Similarly, she would often vacation away from him.

This trip, though, would be different. After World War I broke out in August 1914, Mileva, Hans, and Eduard were unable to travel from Switzerland to Berlin, and they couldn't rejoin Einstein there.

Although the outbreak of World War I may have physically precipitated Albert and Mileva's separation, the seeds of dissatisfaction had probably already been sown. Einstein's increasing fame spurred Mileva's feelings of discontent, and jealousy may have played a role also. It's quite possible she resented his success in light of her own failed career as a scientist. There certainly seems to be a correlation between Einstein's rise in public popularity and Mileva's own personal dissatisfaction with him.

Letters from Albert to Mileva during this time demonstrated that he was becoming increasingly demanding of her time and attention. Their marriage was showing signs of strain, with Einstein insisting that she serve him most meals in his room. He asked her not to speak badly of him in front of their children—although "ask" may be a polite rephrasing of what was actually said—thereby indicating that it was important to Einstein to maintain appearances, even if the situation was quite unhappy in reality.

13. Einstein's second wife Elsa Lowenthal Einstein

In 1912, after a long absence, Einstein became reacquainted with a distant cousin named Elsa Lowenthal. The cousins had gotten together many times during Einstein's youth, when his family still owned a large villa in Munich. By the time they met up in 1912, Elsa had been married (to a man named Max Lowenthal) and had two daughters of her own. Elsa and Einstein were very compatible. Elsa was from a cultural and economic background similar to his, and there was a familiarity between them that didn't exist with Mileva. They enjoyed the same foods and appreciated the same ideals of simple living. Being related, of course, probably contributed to that sense of the familiar. Albert and Elsa began writing letters back and forth, taking a year's hiatus while he attempted to work on his marriage with Mileva. Following this period, however, the letters to Elsa resumed, and they continued to have frequent communication for several years.

Einstein had been separated from his wife starting in 1914, though their divorce was not finalized until 1919. Mileva was not by Einstein's side during the intense period of his illness in 1917. Instead, his cousin Elsa was the one who helped Einstein regain his health. She stood by him completely during this time, and their love grew stronger and stronger. Elsa's caretaking and nursing was likely a factor in Einstein's eventual decision to formalize his separation from Mileva.

$$\Sigma \theta_{\pi\lambda}^{'} \quad \sqrt[\alpha]{\theta} \frac{\sigma}{\Delta} \frac{q}{\pi} \quad \chi \frac{\alpha}{\Delta} \pi \theta_{\Delta} \Sigma \theta_{\pi\lambda}^{'} \quad \sqrt[\alpha]{\theta} \frac{\sigma}{\Delta} \frac{q}{\pi} \chi \frac{\alpha}{\Delta} \pi \Sigma \theta_{\pi\lambda}^{\alpha} \quad \sqrt[\alpha]{\theta} \frac{\sigma}{\Delta} \frac{q}{\pi} \chi \frac{\alpha}{\Delta} \pi \theta_{\Delta}^{\sigma}$$

By 1919, Albert and Mileva's marital discontent (as well as his obvious love for Elsa) reached a point where it could no longer be ignored. Albert and Mileva filed a separation agreement, but Mileva was at first reluctant to divorce him. She probably suspected that he would want to marry Elsa at some point, and her jealousy prompted her to struggle to keep the marriage alive. She eventually conceded, however, and the couple was officially divorced that year.

Einstein didn't exactly sit around in mourning, though. Just a few months after the divorce, Einstein married Elsa Lowenthal. She appears to have been a buffer for his frustrations with Mileva; she both comforted him and provided a familiar, friendly alternative to the tension that existed with Mileva. While Mileva had also been a physicist and could discuss scientific theories with Einstein, Elsa had no such training. While Mileva is rumored to have contributed to Einstein's early theories to at least some extent, it was Elsa who was a better match for Einstein. Rather than competing with him in the scientific arena, she was able to accept that her husband needed solitude and intense concentration to do his work, and she played a supporting role by creating a good working environment for him and placing few demands on him.

Their marriage lasted until Elsa's death in 1936 and, despite Einstein's philandering over the course of his life, appears to have been a happy one. Though they never had children together, Elsa gave Albert the emotional space that perhaps he didn't have with Mileva. The couple traveled together, including a 1922 trip to Japan aboard the steamer *SS Kitano Maru*.

14. EINSTEIN'S STEPDAUGHTERS ILSE AND MARGOT EINSTEIN

In addition to his children from his marriage with Mileva, Albert Einstein had two stepdaughters, Ilse (1897–1934) and Margot (1899–1986). They were Elsa's children from her first marriage. Einstein formally adopted them after his marriage to Elsa, and both legally changed their last name to Einstein. From that point on, their relationship appears to have been very close, and both were a part of the Einstein family. In Einstein's summer house in Caputh (occupied between about 1929 and 1932), both Ilse and Margot had their own rooms.

Albert probably never had the opportunity to know Ilse very well. She died early, in 1934, due to an illness. Rumor had it that, prior to marrying Elsa, Einstein made advances to Ilse, who would have been twenty-two at that time, but there doesn't appear to be much in the way of corroborating evidence. Ilse later married Rudolf Kayser.

Margot, however, became an artist, specializing in sculpture (she actually studied sculpture at Columbia University in the early 1940s). She shared Einstein's fascination with nature and music; when telling stories of her experience in Holland during the Hitler regime, she would often talk about animals instead of people. Perhaps she "inherited" her artistic inclinations from her step-grandmother Pauline, who was a talented musician in her own right.

Rumors have it that Margot may have introduced Einstein to Russian spy Margarita Konenkova in 1935, but not much more is known here. Margot came to live with Einstein in Princeton, New

Jersey, after her move to America. After Elsa's death, Margot took on some of Einstein's secretarial duties, helping to manage his library and other collections. She became something of a public figure around Princeton, getting involved with different committees and organizations. She attended various lectures, enjoyed concerts, and made many friends there.

Toward the end of his life, the Einstein residence was also shared with Johanna Fantova, a Princeton librarian who kept an elaborate diary of Einstein's memoirs. Margot visited the Princeton libraries and museums often, once inviting a curator (Gillet Griffin) to the Einstein house for dinner, and was close friends with Helen Dukas, Einstein's secretary. Margot Einstein died in 1986. Following her death, Einstein's library (consisting of music recordings, scores, books, and other works) was donated to The Jewish National & University Library.

15. EINSTEIN'S GRANDCHILDREN

Hans Albert Einstein (1904-1973) and his first wife Frieda (formerly Frieda Knecht, from Zurich) had three children. Klaus died as a child, but Bernard and Evelyn grew up to have accomplished careers in their own right.

Following in his grandfather's footsteps, Bernard became a physicist. He was also an author, and he wrote a foreword to a book about his grandfather entitled *The Fascinating Life and Theory of Albert Einstein.*

Evelyn Einstein obtained her degree in anthropology and currently resides in Berkeley, California. She is a cult deprogrammer, working with people who have been members of cults. When someone has a relative or friend who has joined a religion or "cult" that they consider to be dangerous or otherwise inappropriate, they may hire a deprogrammer to physically and emotionally separate them from that cult's influence. These sorts of interventions can be conducted in a variety of ways and are often considered controversial.

Evelyn had a somewhat dubious honor, as well. In 1955, Dr. Thomas Harvey, chief pathologist at Princeton University, autopsied Einstein's brain in the hopes of learning about what had gone into creating the genius that was Einstein. Years later, granddaughter Evelyn became the recipient of part of Einstein's brain. If you're interested in more information on this subject, Michael Paterniti has written a book entitled *Driving Mr. Albert: A Trip Across America with Einstein's Brain*.

16. EINSTEIN AND MAJOR HEALTH CRISES

Einstein became seriously ill in 1917. He collapsed, perhaps partly due to pressures from his research and partly from the new stress of being such a prominent figure throughout the scientific community. He'd been working on developing his theory of gravity during this time, and it's likely that he nearly exhausted himself to death. There were, of course, diagnosable medical issues to blame for his collapse as well; this illness seemed to have stemmed from a combination of stomach ulcers and liver trouble. These problems were most likely exacerbated by the food shortages suffered in Berlin during that time, as a result of World War I.

Stomach ulcers, or gastric ulcers, generally occur when part of the stomach's lining becomes inflamed, or a sore develops in the stomach lining. It's possible that bacteria such as H. Pylori may have caused Einstein's gastric ulcers. Other potential causes are excessive alcohol, caffeine, stress, and smoking. Einstein's love of the pipe is well documented; he enjoyed all aspects of smoking a pipe, from choosing the tobacco to loading the briar. While he considered his pipe to be helpful in his thinking and general contemplation of the world around him, it was considerably less useful to his health.

Penicillin was discovered in 1928 by Alexander Fleming (1881–1955), a professor of bacteriology at the University of London. It wasn't patented for mass production until Andrew Moyer did so in 1948. This tremendous invention, which changed the course of disease management worldwide, wasn't available when Einstein fell ill in 1917. Nowadays we have many cures for stomach ulcers, including both antibiotics and medications that reduce the stomach's acid content, thereby letting the ulcer heal.

Elsa Lowenthal, his cousin and childhood friend, came to his side and nursed him through a lengthy recuperation. In fact, he was only partially recovered when his divorce from Mileva (and subsequent marriage to Elsa) became finalized. After this illness, Einstein supposedly had to follow a bland diet for the rest of his life, a proposition to which he had strong objections. His doctors recommended the removal of caffeine and other ulcer-inducing habits from his daily routine, orders which he appears to have followed, though not religiously.

Did Einstein really take his doctor's advice and cut back on his work after this long illness? Not likely . . . he had another collapse in 1928 that was probably the result of long hours and stress (and, perhaps, from his not following the doctor's orders regarding diet). While sailing surely allowed Einstein to get some exercise, he doesn't appear to have sacrificed much by way of diet until later in life. He apparently became a vegetarian in his last years.

Einstein died of an aneurysm (a ruptured artery in his heart) in Princeton, New Jersey, on April 18, 1955. He died in his sleep, at the culmination of a long illness. Einstein chose not to have a funeral or gravestone; he was cremated and his ashes were scattered near a river in New Jersey.

17. EINSTEIN AND PUBLIC SPEAKING

Despite the amount of practice he had in the area, public speaking was never something Einstein looked forward to. There is an anecdote about one of Einstein's solutions to speechmaking. Throughout much of his career, Einstein traveled and gave speeches while his driver sat in the back of the room for each of them. At one point, the driver remarked that, having listened to so many speeches, he could give Einstein's speech almost as well as the original author. So, at the next speech, Einstein sat in the back of the room, and the driver gave the speech—and gave a perfect performance.

During the QA session someone asked a detailed scientific question. After careful contemplation, the driver answered with something like, "Well, that's actually a very simple question, I bet even my driver sitting in the back of the room could answer it."

Was this true? Einstein was such a recognizable figure; wouldn't someone have noticed that Einstein himself wasn't actually standing at the podium?

18. EINSTEIN AND SAILING

Sailing ranked among one of the most important things in Einstein's life (the others were his work and the violin.) He had a life-long interest in aquatic sports, probably dating back to his early days of playing in the lakes surrounding Munich. He had a sailboat at his summer home in Caputh (close to Berlin), which was confiscated by the Nazi's; his house there was stormed after Einstein renounced his German citizenship and left Germany.

During his years at Princeton, Einstein again took up sailing. He often sailed on Lake Carnegie, which was created in 1906 and gave the undergraduate rowers a place to practice. Johanna Fantova, his close personal friend and a former Princeton librarian, kept diaries of Einstein's activities and noted sailing to be one of his favorite pastimes.

Sailing was an excellent output for Einstein's energies, combining mathematics and physics, as well as nautical engineering. Sailing provided both physical activity and mind-clearing freedom; he brought a notebook on all his sailing ventures in order to jot down thoughts. Some of his best thoughts were said to occur while working on his sailboats—while he spent much time actually sailing, he was also said to enjoy simply drifting and cogitating.

He did much of his sailing on Long Island. He was seen all over town in the summers of 1938 and 1939 and was particularly fond of Little Peconic Bay, calling it one of the most beautiful sites he had ever seen. He had his own boat, a 15-foot sailboat named "Tinef" (the word means "junk" or "worthless" in Yiddish). He was said to enjoy sailing as passionately as he enjoyed music.

19. WHAT HAPPENED TO EINSTEIN'S BRAIN?

Einstein died on April 18, 1955, in Princeton, New Jersey. His close friend and advisor, Otto Nathan, was present during his last days, and Einstein trusted him to carry out his wishes after death; Nathan was the executor of Einstein's estate. While Nathan appears not to have given specific permission for an autopsy, Einstein's son Hans Albert allegedly gave permission for Dr. Thomas Harvey, chief pathologist at Princeton University, to conduct an autopsy of Einstein's body. The opportunity to learn about what had gone into creating the genius that was Einstein was too great to pass up, and the decision was made to autopsy Einstein's brain as well.

The brain was removed from the body and was kept by Dr. Harvey at Princeton University. Would Einstein have in fact approved of this research? He was known for saying that he wanted to be cremated because he didn't want people to worship his bones. Dr. Harvey and Hans Albert

Σθ′㼌λ ᵗᶿθ₄ᵍᴨ ᵡᔑᴨ θ∆ Σθ′㼌λ ᵗᶿθ₄ᵍᴨ ᵡᔑᴨ Σθ ᵘ㼌λ ᵗᶿθ₄ᵍᴨ ᵡᔑᴨ θ∆ ᵘ

agreed to keep media coverage at a minimum in order to preserve Einstein's legacy as it was, and not tarnish it with all the attention that would flock to a brain dissection. The initial study consisted of weighing and measuring his brain, then dissecting it into 240 pieces. Oddly, however, Dr. Harvey ended up keeping most of the brain for himself for almost thirty years, only doling out small pieces to other researchers periodically.

Eventually, however, several scientific studies were published on Einstein's brain. A key paper in 1985, "On the Brain of a Scientist: Albert Einstein" [*Experimental Neurology* 88 (1985): 198–204] detailed the ratio of neurons to glial cells. Glial cells surround neurons, providing nourishment and other support. Parts of his brain were said to consist of a higher percentage of glial cells than average, perhaps suggesting that neuron activity in those areas was higher than average. A second paper in 1996 discussed the fact that Einstein's brain weighed less than average (1,230 grams compared to the average 1,400 grams for a male), and also mentioned that Einstein's cerebral cortex was thinner than average. However, based on other data, this paper argued that his brain was unusually neuron-dense, meaning more neurons were active and, potentially, there was greater capacity for mathematical and spatial reasoning.

A third paper in 1999 was published in the British medical journal *The Lancet* [353 (1999): 2149–2153] and described research by Dr. Sandra Wittleson, who showed how Einstein's brain contained unusual patterns of "sulci" (grooves) in the areas of the brain that focus on mathematics. Also, despite the reduced weight, Einstein's brain was 15 percent wider than what is typically seen in other brains. Could this research explain why

Einstein was so skilled in mathematical reasoning? While some scientists can theorize that this may be the case, others will argue that it is difficult to draw such conclusions from the study of only one such genius, and other examples would be needed to verify these findings.

So where is his brain now? Dr. Harvey apparently transported some parts of Einstein's brain around the country with him during his travels. Some pieces went to Dr. Wittleson and other researchers for study. Some sections remain with the pathology department at Princeton Hospital. It is also thought that Einstein's granddaughter Evelyn became the recipient of the remaining pieces.

What was the result of all this scientific experimentation? While Einstein's brain may have deviated slightly from the norm, for the most part, it's not possible to say that the physical structure of his brain was unique enough to have been the sole reason for his achievements. Einstein's brain wasn't enormously different from everybody else's; the factors contributing to his greatness came from both within and outside him.

Part 2

You often take the measure of a man by the company he keeps. When it comes to someone like Albert Einstein, it isn't just about the company he kept during his lifetime, it's about the intellectual company he is grouped with. Einstein's intelligence, determination, and accomplishments have placed him in the pantheon of names we historically associate with the greatest inventors and thinkers.

Newton. Darwin. Da Vinci. Edison. Einstein. Rarified company to be sure. Einstein's associations didn't just include the greatest minds of history. During his life, Einstein was able to work, directly and indirectly, with the leading theorists and researchers of the era; each of them building off of the work of the others, driving science and understanding forward. Though he is easily the most highly regarded and well known, Einstein was influenced as much as he influenced others.

20. EINSTEIN VERSUS GALILEO: THEORIES OF GRAVITY

The first mathematical description of gravity was performed by Italian Galileo Galilei (1564–1642). Galileo, while perhaps best known for his observations with the telescope, also developed the first formulaic description of gravity. In studying gravity, Galileo determined that all objects fall with the same acceleration, no matter what their mass. The motion of a falling body depends on two things: the way in which the body was released, and its initial velocity. Thus, heavy objects fall as fast as lighter objects.

How did Galileo come to these conclusions? Gravity was known from ancient times as an attractive force. However, from the time of the first Greek scientists until the Renaissance, it was thought of as a force that only acted when two objects were touching each other.

Galileo refined this idea by thinking of gravity as a force that attracts any two masses to each other. He did a series of experiments to test his ideas, which involved rolling balls down ramps.

In Galileo's ramp experiments, he rolled balls down a series of ramps that ended above the ground. He then measured the trajectory of the balls after they left the ramp, recording the height at which they were released at the top of the ramp, and the distance they traveled from the bottom of the ramp before hitting the ground.

Galileo also did experiments by dropping objects from a tower. He showed that if he dropped a heavy cannonball and a lighter ball at the same time, they hit the ground at the same time. These experiments showed that the acceleration of gravity is independent of the mass of an object.

Of course, if Galileo had chosen to drop two objects of different shape, such as a feather and a cannonball, they would not have reached the ground at the same time. Why? The answer is air resistance, or drag, which is proportional to the surface area of an object. Two objects with the same shape, but different masses, will reach the ground at the same time. However, since a feather has more surface area than a ball, the feather will take more time to reach the ground than a compact object of the same mass. If two objects are dropped in a vacuum, however, they will reach the ground at the same time, independent of surface area, because there is no drag.

Galileo's experiments showed that the acceleration of gravity was the same for all falling objects and that any two objects would hit the ground at the same time if they were not subject to drag. This overturned previous notions, such as those of Aristotle, which assumed that heavier objects fell faster than lighter ones. Galileo's results, however, were purely experimental. He did not provide an explanation for how gravity worked, or any mathematical basis for his theories. Such mathematical formulations would come later, with the work of Sir Isaac Newton.

Galileo was the first to accurately describe the unyielding attraction of gravity, and his work also led to the first reliable methods of timekeeping. His discoveries allowed the creation of accurate pendulum clocks for the first time, since he found that the period of a pendulum, the time that it takes for one swing to take place, stays the same even as the system loses energy and the height of the pendulum's swing gets smaller. These discoveries paved the way for Newton's laws of motion and gravity, which more accurately and mathematically described the motion of falling objects. However, it was Einstein who eventually disproved both Galileo's view of a universal gravitational force, with the theory of general relativity, and the invariance of time, in the theory of special relativity. Of course, without Galileo's initial discoveries, Newton and Einstein would not have had theories to build on and disprove.

Galileo is primarily famous for his discovery of the four large satellites of Jupiter, the first celestial bodies proven to be orbiting around a planet other than the Earth. This discovery supported the heliocentric model of the solar system, which placed the sun at the center with all the planets orbiting it, eventually leading to its acceptance. Orbital mechanics was thought to be well understood until the nineteenth century, when it was realized that there was an anomaly in the orbit of the planet Mercury. Einstein finally resolved this paradox in 1915 with his theory of general relativity, which allowed for the distortions of space and time that resulted in the observed advance of the perihelion of Mercury.

21. Einstein's response to Isaac Newton

Isaac Newton (1642–1727) developed the laws of motion, leading to the law of universal gravitation. Based on his studies of the motion of the moon around the Earth, Newton was able to formulate a theory of gravitation that applied both to the heavenly bodies and to falling objects on Earth.

Always the critic, Albert Einstein would later displace some of Newton's theories. Of particular interest is that, in his formation of special relativity, Einstein would show that space and time were not absolute. Newton had earlier posited that space and time existed absolutely, despite whatever motion or matter was present. Einstein shattered this theory with his pronouncement of special relativity. Without Newton's theories, however, Einstein wouldn't have had anything to respond to, and his concept of relativity might never have surfaced. The debt Einstein owed to Newton, despite challenging his theories, is enormous.

The lives of Newton and Einstein contained a number of parallels. Both were considered poor students early on, and both were thought to be "slow" by their teachers. Einstein and Newton both had a period of marked genius early on in their scientific careers, and both turned to politics and activism toward the end of their lives.

A major similarity between Einstein and Newton is that both their bodies of work were foundational; their research provided the basis for what would come to be modern science. Both Newton and Einstein wrote formative papers that would both define their work and their legacies. Newton's "Philosophiae Naturalis Principia Mathematica," better known simply as the "Principia," was finished in 1687. It was written in several volumes, including "Of the Motion of Bodies" and "The System of the World." This masterpiece explained Newton's three laws of motion, as well as defining his theory of universal gravitation. Similarly, Einstein wrote three seminal papers in 1905; they were on the photoelectric effect, special relativity, and his formulation of a relationship between mass and energy ($E = mc^2$). These papers became the works Einstein is best known for and helped define his place in history.

Both Einstein and Newton were also interested in a true scientific formulation of gravity. Newton began this study with his law of universal gravity, and Einstein continued the work as he tried to combine gravity with his theory of special relativity. This combination led to the formulation of general relativity. Gravity continues to puzzle scientists today as they continue Einstein's ultimately-unsuccessful quest for a grand unifying theory of physics.

Einstein and Newton were innovators in the truest sense; they used reason and logic to create entirely new ways of viewing the universe. Both set precedents in the field of science and mathematics, and both realized the importance of history in achieving a future.

$$F = ma \qquad \frac{F=Gm_1m_2}{r^2} \qquad \text{compared to } E = mc^2$$

22. SIMILARITIES EINSTEIN DREW FROM DARWINIAN IDEAS

Charles Darwin (1809–1882), a scientist and naturalist, is another historical figure whose impact (like Einstein's) on the world can hardly go unnoticed. Educated in England, Darwin originally decided he wanted to study medicine. Unable to tolerate the idea of performing surgery without anesthesia, however, he switched courses and joined the clergy of the Church of England. He actually received his degree in this field. The important thing here is to realize that, in relation to Einstein, Darwin had an early education in science and religion, both of which would be critical to his later work.

In 1831 Darwin was invited to go on a scientific expedition aboard the *H.M.S. Beagle*. He was asked to be part of the trip to South America as a naturalist and remained a part of this expedition for five years. While in South America, he found fossils of animals that were presently extinct, but bore marked similarities to modern creatures. He studied plants and animals from all over South America, particularly the Galapagos Islands.

When he returned to London, Darwin formalized his observations from the trip in his work "On the Origin of Species by Means of Natural Selection," published in 1859 and revised a number of times. Not only was he convinced that evolution existed, he believed that it occurred gradually. Evolution occurred through "natural selection," a process by which those most fit to survive, will; everything else will not. Additionally, he suggested that all species evolved from one life form through "specialization."

The four main tenets of Darwin's "On the Origin of Species by Means of Natural Selection":

1. Evolution exists.
2. Evolution takes place slowly, over millions of years.
3. Evolution occurs through natural selection.
4. All species evolved from a single life form.

Needless to say, Darwin's theory of evolution created strong currents in both the scientific and religious communities. Natural science and physical explanations were suggested as a driving force behind human development. This idea is clearly in contrast with the Western religious notion of a God having created the Earth, the heavens, and all living creatures. Although Darwin himself avoided creating a direct conflict between creation and evolution, others would soon draw the comparison.

While the lives of Darwin and Einstein did not cross paths significantly (Einstein was born in 1879, three years before Darwin's death), there is a historical commonality between these two great scientists. Both Darwin and Einstein would serve as representatives, in a way. The field of evolutionary biology basically formed itself around Darwin and his theories, much as the field of modern theoretical physics blossomed around Einstein. Neither Darwin nor Einstein created their respective fields; however, they brought their ideas into both political and social consciousness, and thus became icons.

$\Sigma\theta^{\gamma}_{\;\pi\lambda}$ $^{\sigma}\!\theta_{\Delta}\!{}^{\sigma}_{\pi}$ $^{\chi}\!\Delta^{\pi}\theta_{\Delta}\Sigma\theta^{\epsilon}_{\;\pi\lambda}$ $^{\sigma}\!\theta_{\Delta}\!{}^{\sigma}_{\pi}$ $^{\chi}\!\Delta^{\pi}\Sigma\theta^{\;\alpha}_{\;\pi\lambda}$ $^{\sigma}\!\theta_{\Delta}\!{}^{\sigma}_{\pi}$ $^{\chi}\!\Delta^{\pi}\theta_{\Delta}^{\;\sigma}$

One of the differences between Darwin and Einstein, however, comes in their views of spirituality. Darwin's theory of evolution was a direct challenge to religious views of the origin of humans and animals on Earth, and in fact one of his goals was to find a scientific explanation for the biological diversity that exists on Earth today, without resorting to a "Creator". While Einstein's views on religion and spirituality did not follow any particular orthodox mindset, he was known to believe in a general order of the universe. This notion has been referred to as the "scientist's God." A famous quote describing Einstein's objection to quantum mechanics, which reduces subatomic behavior to probabilities rather than certainties, was that "God does not play dice with the universe."

While both Darwin and Einstein attempted to find scientific theories to explain the observable details of the world around them, biology in Darwin's case and physics in Einstein's, Darwin's work was hindered by the lack of testable hypotheses. The scientific method depends on making predictions that can then be tested and either proven correct or incorrect. Even many of Einstein's seemingly most outlandish predictions, such as the existence of black holes, were eventually proved correct by experimental results. Darwin's theory of evolution, however, was much more difficult to test because it deals with gradual change over hundreds of millions of years, something that is very difficult to simulate in a laboratory. Perhaps because of this difficulty, Darwin's theory (while currently accepted by most evolutionary biologists) is still challenged by those in the creationist camp, while Einstein's theories have largely been accepted.

23. EINSTEIN AND THE WRIGHT BROTHERS

The Wright brothers, Orville and Wilbur, will be known throughout history as the inventors of the airplane. The turn of the twentieth century was a great time to be an inventor, and the Wrights had plenty of competition. In 1891, a German inventor, Otto Lilienthal (1848–1896), worked on developing hang gliders. He actually attempted powered flights, but died in a glider accident in 1896. There were many other European attempts to create the first powered airplane during these years.

The Wright brothers were right in the thick of things. They built and tested their first glider in Kitty Hawk, North Carolina in 1900. They built their first powered airplane in 1903 and made their first successful flight on December 17, 1903. The significance of this flight is that it was the first heavier-than-air powered flight that was also manned. Additionally, in these years they patented their method of providing lateral control while flying and continued to create better and more powerful planes. They would make more record-breaking flights in France in 1908.

What ultimately set them apart from their contemporaries is that they persisted and had consistent successes that improved upon their past work. They studied and read about flight as much as possible and were experts in aeronautical history. They didn't conduct blind experiments; they were acutely aware of what had worked in the past and, perhaps more importantly, what had not worked. Their work was greatly admired during their own time, to the point where many other inventors copied (some would say stole) their ideas and built planes of their own, often without paying adequate respect or fees to the Wright brothers.

Were the Wright brothers geniuses on Einstein's level? Probably not. Neither seems to have been an outstanding student, nor did they appear to have had a natural capacity that went above and beyond. What set the Wright brothers apart was their incredible devotion to and aptitude for flying. They studied voraciously, digested what they read, interpreted as necessary, and came up with their own successful ideas. Like Einstein, they kept plugging away at their work until they achieved the desired result. Also like Einstein, they made their mark in history by being the first to force society's awareness of their special area of interest, and the Wright brothers and Einstein both transformed the path that modern life would take.

Genius, then, comes in many shapes and forms. Some geniuses possess incredible intelligence, others diligence. Some display aptitude in a number of different areas. All contribute to history in a way that can be imitated, but never replaced. Einstein perhaps represents the best possible combination of these elements.

24. How was Einstein like Edison?

Like Einstein, Thomas Alva Edison (1847–1931) is another famous scientist who had to deal with disabilities over the course of his lifetime. He was born slightly deaf, like Alexander Graham Bell, and his early teachers thought him to be on the slow side. Of course, nothing could have been further from the truth. Probably because of his hearing problem, he didn't pay attention in school as well as his teachers would have liked; it's possible that his inability to focus was related to what we today call Attention Deficit Disorder. Not that it stopped him, or even slowed him down—Edison set up a laboratory in the basement of his parents' house and published his first newspaper at the age of twelve.

Edison is probably most famous for his 1879 invention of the incandescent electric light bulb. In 1883 Edison created the framework for the first system of generating power, heat, and electric light; his Edison General Electric Company would become the General Electric Corporation in 1892. He produced an amazing number of other inventions over the course of his life. Notable examples include a phonograph, an electric pen, and the mimeograph machine. He had more than 1,000 patents granted during his life, an absolutely phenomenal number. Edison is one of history's most prolific inventors, and that he had learning and physical disabilities did nothing to damper his enthusiasm.

Edison's hearing problem grew worse as time went on, and he would eventually become completely deaf in his left ear. However, Edison learned to live with and even embrace his disability; he thought that not being able to hear gave him the ability to concentrate on his work more than "normal" people could. Even when surgery that could have helped his hearing loss became available later in his life, he refused it. This aspect of Edison's character was similar, in a way, to Einstein's; both took advantage of the fact that they weren't just like everybody else, and both triumphed beyond all expectation.

The most significant and obvious comparison to Einstein is that Edison was one of the most prolific scientists of his era. He produced more significant inventions than anyone else in his field. Can you imagine your life without electricity? Without refrigerated food, lighting, computers, or anything else that gets plugged into an outlet? Not a pretty picture. Similarly, most of us wouldn't want to go through life without recorded music; Edison's invention of the phonograph paved the way for the cassettes, CDs, and DVDs that are ubiquitous today.

25. How was Einstein like Leonardo da Vinci?

To take a step further back in time, Leonardo da Vinci (1452–1519) is yet another example of a famous scientist who didn't allow a disability to stifle his work. Da Vinci was born in Anchiano, Italy during the Renaissance. He was a curious child, questioning everything and everyone around him.

Da Vinci had his first internship with Andrea del Verrocchio in 1466. With del Verrocchio, he learned sculpture, painting, metalworking, and other artistic skills. Da Vinci would open his own workshop in the following years and earned his own commissions for paintings and drawings. He would create some of the Renaissance's most famous works, including the *Mona Lisa* and *The Last Supper.*

While often remembered most for his painting, da Vinci was a true Renaissance figure. He used his skills in math and science to develop linear perspective in his two-dimensional work, and these advances would

$\Sigma \theta^{\iota}_{\pi\Delta}{}^{\lambda}$ "$^{\sigma}_{\pi}\theta$ "$\pi\theta\Delta\Sigma\theta^{\iota}_{\pi\Delta}{}^{\lambda}$ "$^{\sigma}_{\pi}\theta\frac{\sigma}{\Delta}\pi^{\chi}\Delta^{\pi}\Sigma\theta^{\iota}_{\pi\Delta}{}^{\lambda}$ "$^{\sigma}_{\pi}\theta\frac{\sigma}{\Delta}\pi^{\chi}\Delta^{\pi}\theta\Delta$ "

form the basis for many future breakthroughs in various artistic fields. In his later years, da Vinci devoted more of his time to engineering. He actually worked on a project to re-channel the course of the Arno River. Like Einstein, then, da Vinci applied his immense intelligence and skill to many different areas of interest.

Another similarity between Einstein and da Vinci is that both were reputed to have learning disabilities. Einstein was late in learning to speak and was reputed to have had trouble expressing himself in writing throughout his career. Not that this problem stopped him from making incredible discoveries. He was also, of course, known for his more popular quotations, such as "Imagination is more important than knowledge" and "Gravitation is not responsible for people falling in love."

Leonardo da Vinci is thought to have had a learning disability, dyslexia, which is a condition that makes it difficult for people to learn to read and write. It says nothing of someone's natural intelligence, but can make primary school education a particularly trying process, especially in the fifteenth century when not much was known about this condition. Did his dyslexia slow da Vinci down? Not a chance. It was, however, a fairly significant part of his legacy. Most of da Vinci's handwritten notes that survive today were written backwards. He lettered from right-to-left, as a mirror image of what normal text would be. Many dyslexics share this interesting anomaly, and most aren't aware that they're doing it. This aspect of da Vinci's professional life certainly didn't seem to affect his ability to produce masterpieces that would be some of the greatest ever created.

Like Einstein, Leonardo da Vinci created world-changing masterpieces. Though their chosen fields were far apart from each other, there was actually some crossover. At various points in his career da Vinci played inventor, creating designs for buildings, machinery, airplanes, canals, and many more (and varied) items. Einstein also had the inventor's streak, producing designs for a noiseless refrigerator, among others; he held several patents for various other inventions, including a gyrocompass and a special airplane gyrocompass. This similarity begs the question: are all geniuses also inventors? Is there something about great minds that drives them to create?

26. HOW WAS EINSTEIN LIKE MICHELANGELO?

Michelangelo Buonarroti (1475–1564) was one of the most prolific artists of the Renaissance. He was skilled in painting, sculpture, poetry, architecture—the list goes on. The "genius" label is generally attributed to Michelangelo for the quality and creativity of his work, but also for the number of different aspects of art that he affected. He would influence the entire course of Western art.

Born in Caprese, a small village in Italy, Michelangelo spent most of his life working in Florence and Rome. In the Renaissance tradition, Michelangelo studied in the workshops of the masters, learning by internship from those who had already succeeded. He studied painting first under the tutelage of Domenico Ghirlandaio, and then studied sculpture in the Medici gardens. In 1498 he produced one of his first

$\Sigma \theta^{\chi}_{\overline{J\Delta}} \lambda \,^{\prime\prime}\!\overline{J}\!\theta \qquad \,^{\prime\prime}\pi\,\theta_{\Delta}\,\Sigma\theta^{\chi}_{\overline{J\Delta}}\lambda \,^{\prime\prime}\!\overline{J}\!\theta\frac{\sigma}{\Delta}\!\overline{J}\pi^{\chi}\Delta\pi\,\Sigma\theta\,^{\alpha}_{\overline{J\Delta}}\lambda \,^{\prime\prime}\!\overline{J}\!\theta\frac{\sigma}{\Delta}\!\overline{J}\pi^{\chi}\Delta\pi\,\theta_{\Delta}\,^{\alpha}$

large-scale sculptures, the *Bacchus*, and, in 1500, he completed *Pieta* for St. Peter's Basilica in Rome.

Returning to Florence, he completed his famous *David* statue in 1504. Choice of subject matter, attention to facial expression, and amazing detail made this one of his most famous works. Michelangelo was called back to Rome in 1505 to work on frescoes for the Sistine Chapel ceiling. His career in architecture took off shortly thereafter; he designed the tomb for Julius II around 1515, the Laurentian Library in the 1520s, and the Medici Tombs between 1519 and 1534.

At this point he took a break from architecture to work on what was probably his most famous painting, *The Last Judgment*, between 1536 and 1541. After the completion of this work he returned to architecture. During this later period of his life, he created some of his signature works such as the Campidoglio (the Roman capitol building) and the Dome at St. Peters, his most famous architectural achievement. His last years were spent on frescoes for the Pauline Chapel in the Vatican.

Though Michelangelo predated Einstein by some 300 years, their lives followed similar paths to greatness. Like Einstein, Michelangelo was incredibly prolific. To some extent, Michelangelo's achievement is more comprehensible—scientific research is a difficult field for producing lots of results on demand. Another similarity is that Einstein's research crossed many interdisciplinary borders and boundaries, much like Michelangelo's.

Michelangelo had the advantage of being historically placed right in the middle of the Italian Renaissance (approximately 1420–1600). Italy was one of the focal points of this amazingly prolific period; the developments and achievements of this period went on to influence the entire course of art, science, and politics, and Michelangelo was both a contributor and an absorber of this culture. Similarly, Einstein was theorizing about science and physics as the Industrial Revolution (approximately 1700–1900) was coming to an end; great mechanized inventions were developing and becoming more common, and Einstein was surrounded by the influx of new technology.

Also like Einstein, Michelangelo was recognized as a genius during his own time. Michelangelo's work was acknowledged at the time as being inspired and amazingly well-executed, and history remembers his work in much the same way. Michelangelo was one of the most sought-after artists of the Renaissance for precisely this reason—his reputation preceded him and actually earned him many commissions. Similarly, most people knew Einstein's name during his lifetime because his achievements were of such monumental importance, and Einstein certainly had no lack of job opportunities.

27. EINSTEIN AND BAUHAUS

In 1924, Einstein played a role in the creation and continuance of one of the period's most important architectural movements. The Bauhaus School (Staatliches Bauhaus in German) was a daring new school of architecture and design that was founded in 1919. Bauhaus design principles influenced most aspects of life—furniture design, photography, typeface, theater, use of color, architectural style, and kitchen dishes just to name a few. It led to the architectural Modernism movement, which was characterized not only by physical buildings but also by the cantilevering and clean designs that were applied to furniture and art. Many Bauhaus students and instructors would go on to become famous. Some of the more well known alumni include Wassily Kandinsky, Marcel Breuer, Paul Klee, and Ludwig Mies van der Rohe.

Walter Gropius headed the school, which was founded in Weimar, Germany (and was actually sponsored by the Weimar Republic for several years). Gropius' idea was that, with the end of World War I, an entirely new period of history was coming into place, and this era should be reflected in the culture of the day. Gropius would eventually have a worldwide impact on architecture—he served as the chair of Harvard University's Graduate School of Design in 1937. The Bauhaus School relocated to Dessau, Germany, in 1925. The death of the school came at the hands of the Nazis in 1933, and many of its teachers moved to the United States at that time. The Nazi regime opposed the Bauhaus movement (and many other movements), accusing it of being a

Communist movement simply because it had some Russian members. Nazi misinterpretation severely limited the growth of artistic (not to mention religious) development, making it all too clear how important freedom of expression really is.

During that difficult time, Einstein came out in support of this radical new style, and his endorsement helped the school gain popularity. Also a victim of Nazi terror and discrimination, Einstein felt a distinct sympathy with the goals of the Bauhaus movement. One of the main purposes of Bauhaus was to bring together arts and technology; similarly, Einstein believed in unifying physics, mathematics, and space into large overarching theories. In fact, in 1924 a group called the "Friends of the Bauhaus Society" was formed, and Einstein was a leading member. Other supporters included composer Arnold Schönberg and artist Marc Chagall.

Einstein had direct relationships with Bauhaus artisans. When building his Caputh summer home in 1929, Einstein commissioned Bauhaus architect Konrad Wachsmann for the task (Wachsmann went on to work directly with Walter Gropius in the 1940s). Einstein wanted the home to be simple and practical; Wachsmann responded by using a prefabricated wooden construction system with built-in cabinets and large windows, hallmarks of the Bauhaus movement. The two became good friends, with Einstein actually helping Wachsmann emigrate to the United States in 1941.

28. EINSTEIN AT ODDS WITH MAXWELL OVER ELECTROMAGNETISM

The history of science is one where a series of giants stand on each other's shoulders to achieve greatness. Isaac Newton formulated the basics of motion and gravity; Charles Coulomb's work with electromagnetism preceded Michael Faraday, whose work allowed James Maxwell to arrive at his conclusions. Einstein then built off of Maxwell's ideas to formulate relativity. Talk about a chain of intelligence.

James Maxwell (1831–1879) was a Scottish physicist and mathematician. By the time he was fourteen, Maxwell was generating mathematical equations for geometric shapes, and he studied the writings of Newton extensively.

Maxwell continued Faraday's work in the definition of electromagnetism. In 1856, he published a paper entitled "On Faraday's Lines of Force," in which he applied mathematics (never Faraday's strong suit) to some of Faraday's theories. Maxwell's major contribution to Faraday's work was the idea that at the core of electromagnetism is the concept of the electromagnetic field.

There were, Maxwell posited, two main types of electromagnetic fields: stationary and changing. A static field was one where the field itself remained bound to its origin; an example would be the type of magnetic field generated around a wire conducting electrical current. The other type of electromagnetic field would be a changing field, where the field takes on a wave motion as it propagates. Radio waves, gamma rays, x-rays, and microwaves are all examples of changing electromagnetic fields, whose waves travel at the speed of light.

One of Maxwell's most significant contributions to science was the idea that light, electricity, and magnetism were fundamentally just different manifestations of related concepts. Maxwell codified his thinking with "Maxwell's equations," four major ways of describing the way electricity and magnetism relate to each other. These equations are actually partial differential equations, and they describe the complex interdependencies between charges, density, and the electric field. These equations are inherently complex and difficult to understand; the important part, though, is that they describe electromagnetic radiation.

Maxwell's equations are as follows (expressed in macroscopic, differential form, standard MKS units):

- Charge density and the electric field: $\nabla \cdot D = \rho$
- Structure of the magnetic field: $\nabla \cdot B = 0$
- A changing magnetic field and the electric field:
  $\nabla \times E = -\partial B/\partial t$
- Source of the magnetic field: $\nabla \times H = J + \partial D/\partial t$
- H = magnetic field strength
- J = current density
- ρ = electrical charge density
- D = electric displacement field
- E = electrical field

$$\Sigma\theta^{\dot{\tau}}_{\pi\lambda}{}^{\alpha\dot{\lambda}}_{\theta} \qquad {}^{\alpha}\pi\,\theta_{\Delta}\Sigma\theta^{\dot{\tau}}_{\pi\lambda}{}^{\alpha\dot{\lambda}}_{\theta}\frac{\sigma}{4}\pi{}^{\chi}\Delta^{\delta}\pi\Sigma\theta{}^{\alpha}_{\pi\lambda}{}^{\alpha\dot{\lambda}}_{\theta}\frac{\sigma}{4}\pi{}^{\chi}\Delta^{\delta}\pi\,\theta_{\Delta}{}^{\alpha}$$

B = magnetic flux

t = time

∇ = del (a mathematical function made up of partial derivatives)

Inconsistencies in Maxwell's equations led to the eventual formation of Einstein's theories. By all accounts, electromagnetism as defined by Maxwell would become a precursor to relativity. However, there were some fundamental aspects of Maxwell's theory with which Einstein later took issue. One of the major issues was that Maxwell, in his description of light as a wave, ended up with a fixed speed at which light traveled, regardless of how the light source moved. Einstein would raise the important issue of how this speed was being defined (that is, with respect to what?), and his concept of relativity would spring from this basic discrepancy.

By the end of the nineteenth century, therefore, both Maxwell's elegant, orderly formulations of electromagnetism and Newton's classical mechanics were being questioned. A few seemingly small inconsistencies had been noted, and try as they might, scientists were unable to explain them satisfactorily. Maxwell's equations, which unified the study of electricity, magnetism, and optics (by including light as an electromagnetic wave), showed that the speed of light was a fixed constant. However, the presence of a fixed velocity for light is not compatible with the views of Galileo and Newton, who stated that speed varies depending on the observer. Newton's laws of motion suggest that if an observer in motion measures the speed of light, it should be different from the speed measured by an observer who is at rest. However, Maxwell's equations required a fixed speed of light that does not vary, no matter who is observing it. Sound confusing? It is, and Einstein came along at just the right time to provide some clarity.

Einstein's theory of special relativity solved this paradox, but in a very unexpected way. Most scientists before Einstein had tried to alter Maxwell's equations, by suggesting that an imperceptible "ether" existed that light waves traveled through and that the speed of light was measured relative to this ether. The ether theory caused more problems than it solved, however. Einstein found a different way to resolve the paradox of the speed of light—he proposed that the speed of light in fact did remain constant, but that space and time themselves varied as observed by different viewers. Time dilation and length contraction, two strange consequences of the theory of special relativity, explain how the speed of light can be a constant, but seem to change as observed by viewers in motion (who in fact experience changes in space-time).

29. EINSTEIN'S COLLABORATIONS WITH FERMI

Enrico Fermi (1901–1954), best known for his research into beta decay, was an Italian-American scientist. Fermi was celebrated as both a noted theoretical physicist and a talented experimentalist, a rare combination. He was born in Rome and received his doctorate degree in physics from the University of Pisa at the age of twenty-one.

Fermi first met Einstein in 1924, in Leiden, Netherlands. During this time, Fermi was working on the newly developing field of quantum theory and statistical mechanics. In 1924, Einstein expanded on a theory of Satyendra Nath Bose's to generalize a method of counting the various states of atoms, predicting the existence of Bose-Einstein condensates. This work came to be known as Bose-Einstein statistics. In 1926, Fermi published a paper, independent of Einstein's work, which had a new method to discuss the thermodynamic behavior of a group of electrons. This work came to be known as Fermi–Dirac statistics. The two competing descriptions were integrated in late 1926 by Paul Adrien Maurice Dirac, who described the symmetric relationship between Bose-Einstein and Fermi–Dirac particles.

After he was awarded the Nobel Prize in physics in 1938, Fermi immigrated to the United States to escape the racial laws of Fascism that affected Fermi's wife, Laura Capon, who was Jewish. The Fascist government of Italy had given the Fermis permission to travel to Sweden to accept the Nobel Prize, and they secretly planned to escape to the United States immediately following the ceremony, never to return to Italy.

Fermi began working at Columbia University, in New York, on nuclear physics. In 1939, Fermi, Leo Szilard, and Eugene Wigner realized the danger to the United States if scientists in Hitler's Germany were able to harness a nuclear chain reaction to produce an atomic bomb, and they wrote a letter to President Franklin D. Roosevelt outlining their concerns and suggesting the establishment of an American project to attempt to harness nuclear energy. The letter was also signed by Einstein, who delivered it in person to President Roosevelt on October 11, 1939. As a result of this letter, Columbia University was awarded initial funding to investigate nuclear reactions, which grew into the Manhattan Project in 1942.

Fermi moved to the University of Chicago in the early 1940s, and in 1942, he led a team of scientists who created the world's first self-sustaining nuclear chain reaction. This work took place in a laboratory converted from an old squash court in the basement of the University of Chicago's Stagg Field. Fermi's work on controlled nuclear reactions led directly to the first test of a nuclear device in New Mexico in 1945 and the dropping of two atomic bombs on Hiroshima and Nagasaki a few weeks later.

Fermi's work on controlled nuclear reactions led to the harnessing of nuclear fission in nuclear power plants, and his first experiment in 1942 was in fact a precursor of modern nuclear reactors. While his experiments were harnessed for a terrible wartime purpose, they also led to the development of a powerful new energy source for peacetime.

30. EINSTEIN'S DEBATES WITH BOHR

As the probabilistic description of quantum mechanics (led by Niels Bohr and other scientists) gained in popularity, it also had its critics. Einstein in particular was very resistant to the increased presence of probabilities in the results. He was also uncomfortable with the idea that physical systems only existed when they were observed and that the act of observing made a fundamental change in the state of a system.

$\Sigma\theta'\frac{i}{\pi\Delta}\lambda\ °\frac{\lambda}{\pi\theta}$ $°\pi\,\theta_\Delta\Sigma\theta'\frac{\prime}{\pi\Delta}\lambda\ °\frac{\lambda}{\pi\theta}\Delta_\pi^\sigma\chi\,\Delta^\pi\Sigma\theta\,°\frac{u}{\pi}\lambda\ °\frac{\lambda}{\pi\theta}\Delta_\pi^\sigma\chi\,\Delta^\pi\theta_\Delta\,°$

Einstein believed that natural systems existed on their own, independent of any observations that might be made. He believed that the motions of particles could be exactly calculated based on previous information about them. Einstein was also very uncomfortable with the fact that the theory meant that there was no way to predict exactly when an atom would emit a photon, for example.

Two famous debates on quantum mechanics took place at the Solvay Conferences, held in 1927 and 1930. On these occasions, Bohr and Einstein got into a series of discussions over the details of the new quantum theory. Einstein raised many objections during these debates, and both men went over and over various points of the theory. Even after these discussions, which went on day and night, neither would admit defeat.

The Bohr-Einstein debates served to clarify and strengthen the new description of quantum mechanics. They also led to a paper Einstein wrote in 1935, along with Boris Podolsky and Nathan Rosen. In that paper, entitled "Can Quantum Mechanical Description of Physical Reality Be Considered Complete?" the authors attempted to discredit quantum mechanics by showing a seemingly impossible situation: a measurement of a particle at one location would also reveal information about a particle at a different location. This possibility was called "spooky action at a distance," and actually caused Bohr to back down on one particular point in his formulation of quantum mechanics. However, much later, in 1964, a flaw was found in the Einstein-Podolsky-Rosen formulation showing that matter did indeed behave just as strangely as the three authors had suggested it could not.

$\Sigma \theta^{\iota} \pi^{\lambda} \lambda$ $\sigma^{\eta} \theta \Lambda^{\sigma}_{\Sigma} \pi$ $\chi \Delta^{\sigma} \pi \theta \Lambda \Sigma \theta^{\iota}_{\pi^{\lambda}} \lambda$ $\sigma^{\eta} \theta \Lambda^{\sigma}_{\Sigma} \pi \chi \Delta^{\sigma} \pi \Sigma \theta^{\alpha}_{\pi^{\lambda}} \lambda$ $\sigma^{\eta} \theta \Lambda^{\sigma}_{\Sigma} \pi \chi \Delta^{\prime\prime} \pi \theta \Lambda^{\alpha}$

Expressing his discomfort with the probabilistic nature of quantum theory, Einstein made a famous comment that said, in effect, "God does not play dice with the universe." It is reported that Bohr responded by saying that Einstein should stop telling God what to do.

By the late 1930s, however, Einstein accepted that while quantum mechanics was not perfect, it did at least present a consistent picture of sub-atomic structure and behavior. While classical physics produces satisfactory results for most everyday observations, quantum theory is necessary when observing matter at very small scales, just as relativity proves necessary at very high speeds or large masses.

Einstein never fully accepted quantum mechanics as a complete, finished product. He was still uncomfortable with the fact that the mathematical structure of quantum theory could not predict individual events, but only overall probability. Einstein believed that there must be a simpler, more fundamental, way to describe how each individual atom behaved now and would behave in the future. Einstein began the search for such a theory as an extension of the theory of relativity. It would be this ultimately unsuccessful search for a more basic theory, a unified field theory, which would occupy most of the rest of his life.

Einstein was not the only scientist to try to develop a unified field theory. Other physicists working at about the same time had similar interests. Their main discoveries, though, were in other aspects of science and physics. Erwin Schrödinger (1887-1961) and Werner Heisenberg (1901-1976) were two scientists whose work would be fundamental to the furthering of Einstein's thinking in terms of a unified field theory.

31. THE OLYMPIA ACADEMY

Perhaps even more important than the general knowledge Einstein acquired at the Eidgenössische/Technische/Hochshule (ETH), his polytechnical schooling gave Einstein the ability to come up with ideas about electrodynamics and then to design experiments that would prove his theories. An unproven idea doesn't carry the same weight that a proven theory does, and Einstein recognized this fact. At the ETH he learned how to substantiate his own research, an incredibly important skill for a scientist to have. The work he began at the ETH in electrodynamics would stay with him through his first papers on relativity, and it's probably fair to say that the course of his life wouldn't have been the same without this style of education.

After graduation, Einstein's stint at the patent office certainly wasn't without benefits. He walked home from the patent office each day with his ETH classmate Michele Besso, an Italian–Swiss friend with whom he collaborated on scientific writings in 1913 concerning the motion of Mercury's perihelion. Besso and Einstein reportedly discussed various interesting scientific problems on their walks.

Since at this time Einstein was without the framework of formal scientific collaboration that he would have had with a university posting, he created his own academic environment. In 1902, he placed an ad in the newspaper of the city of Bern, Switzerland, advertising his services as a private tutor in physics and math. The first person to answer his ad was Maurice Solovine, a young Romanian philosopher.

Starting at their first meeting, however, the two came to a quick realization—they preferred debating and discussing philosophy and physics together, rather than Einstein tutoring Solovine in a more formal teacher-student relationship.

Einstein and Solovine were soon joined by another interested party, the mathematician Conrad Habicht. The three became fast friends and called their little group (semi-jokingly) the Olympia Academy. Over time, others joined the group for short periods, including Einstein's soon-to-be wife, Mileva Maric (who apparently didn't participate much, preferring instead to listen); Conrad's brother Paul Habicht; Lucien Chavan, a technician; Einstein's close friend Michele Besso; and Marcel Grossmann, another friend of Einstein's.

The meetings of the Academy included lectures and debates on various subjects, given by the participants. The format was informal and usually started with a dinner; the participants would then begin their lively debates, which often lasted until the wee hours of the morning. They read not only scientific texts, but also philosophical works such as those by Ernst Mach, John Stuart Mill, David Hume, and Spinoza. The participants sometimes even discussed literature, such as Don Quixote by Cervantes.

The Academy was only in existence for a few years, until Conrad Habicht left Bern in 1904. However, it seems to have been a formative scientific experience for Einstein, and one he recalled fondly all his life. The three main founders continued to remain in touch throughout their lives. Einstein in particular seemed to have felt that the experience of lively and vigorous scientific-philosophical debate helped provide a firm foundation for his upcoming scientific career and certainly positioned him well for the three groundbreaking papers he was to publish just a year later in 1905.

32. EINSTEIN'S LETTERS TO FREUD

At first glance, it might seem as if Einstein's physics and Freud's psycho-analysis have little in common. While Einstein would have been consid-ered a "hard" scientist (meaning one who studied physics, chemistry, and so on), he nevertheless had tremendous respect for Freud's work on the subconscious, and the two were in direct communication.

Like Einstein, Sigmund Freud (1856–1939) was also born Jewish, although Freud later declared himself to be an atheist. Freud was born in Austria-Hungary, but he moved to Vienna as a child, staying there until the Nazi occupation in the late 1930s. He studied medicine in school; although he would have preferred a career in research, he also needed a way to earn a living. He decided to obtain a specialty in neurology and go into private practice.

Freud learned about hypnotism from a physician named Josef Breuer; this method would become known as the "talking cure." Although Freud tried the hypnosis method himself, he found patients responded much bet-ter to relaxing on a couch and being asked to talk about whatever came into their minds. This method came to be called "free association," and it was one of the hallmarks of Freud's therapy.

$$\Sigma\theta^{\prime}\frac{\iota}{\pi\lambda}\,\,{}^{\alpha}\gamma\theta\Delta^{\sigma}_{\Sigma}\pi\,\,\chi\Delta^{\ddot\alpha}\pi\,\theta\Delta\,\Sigma\theta^{\prime}\frac{\iota}{\pi\lambda}\,\,{}^{\alpha}\gamma\theta\Delta^{\sigma}_{\Sigma}\pi\,\chi\,\Delta^{\ddot\alpha}\pi\Sigma\theta\,\,{}^{\alpha}_{\pi\lambda}\,\,{}^{\alpha}\gamma\theta\Delta^{\sigma}_{\Sigma}\pi\,\chi\,\Delta^{\ddot\alpha}\pi\,\theta\Delta^{\,\,\alpha}$$

Freud, who was interested in uncovering past trauma as the root of people's current suffering, published his ideas in 1900 in *The Interpretation of Dreams*. He was one of the first to promote the idea of the unconscious mind, one that would retain information but allow that information to resurface in different forms. Although today many of us take his psychological research for granted, these theories were new at the beginning of the twentieth century. Freud had a tremendous impact on the burgeoning field of psychology— he was a prolific writer, and his name soon became a household word.

Like practically everyone else in that time, Einstein was aware of Freud's research, and he recognized that factors other than genetics contributed to what a person would become. He encouraged Freud's exploration of the relatively new field of psychology, and he even included Freud when organizing a meeting of worldwide intellectual leaders, showing how greatly he admired Freud's research.

These two great thinkers subsequently corresponded on a variety of subjects. At one point, Einstein wrote to Freud concerning war. He was curious to know what someone who studied the human psyche thought about the concept of war. Einstein raised an interesting question: Why do world leaders persist in initiating conflict, despite the terrible after-effects? Freud, while not able to provide a reasonable answer for such a question, responded with the observation that the intellectual struggle over war was between might and right; Freud suggested that the controversy was actually between violence and right. He reasoned that humanity, since its inception, protected its rights through sheer violence and that this individual instinct transferred itself to the larger community.

Being inherently violent creatures, humans eagerly assimilated the concept of personal defense and, per Freud's argument, willingly accepted a larger field of conquering and domination. The human impulse is a violent one; much as one body could live by fighting off infectious diseases, a group of people had to survive by battling against and defeating human invaders. To Freud, it was all a matter of instinct and scale. Einstein and Freud communicated many times in the early 1930s, and their letters detail their mutual interest in the nature of man and its corresponding effects on war and peace.

During these tumultuous years, Einstein was developing his idea for a world government. He saw a global governing body as the only means by which to avoid individual nations going to war with each other. It's very interesting that Einstein respected a "soft" scientist such as Freud enough to use him as a sounding board for working out these theories.

33. EINSTEIN'S RELATIONSHIP WITH MARIE CURIE

Marie Sklodowska Curie (1867-1934) was born in Poland in 1867, twelve years before Einstein. She was the daughter of a teacher and was exposed to scientific training in her early school years. She moved to Paris in 1891, studying mathematics and physics there. She received a doctorate degree in 1903 and became a Professor of General Physics at the Sorbonne in 1906—

$\Sigma\theta^{'}_{\pi\lambda}$ $\sqrt[\alpha]{\theta}\mathcal{L}^{\sigma}_{\pi}$ $\chi^{\Delta}_{\pi}\theta_{\Delta}$ $\Sigma\theta^{'}_{\pi\lambda}$ $\sqrt[\alpha]{\theta}\mathcal{L}^{\sigma}_{\pi}\chi^{\Delta}_{\pi}\Sigma\theta^{''}_{\pi\lambda}$ $\sqrt[\alpha]{\theta}\mathcal{L}^{\sigma}_{\pi}\chi^{\Delta}_{\pi}\theta_{\Delta}^{''}$

she was their first female professor. She married Professor Pierre Curie (1859–1906) , a physics professor, in 1895, but he unfortunately died in 1906.

The Curies performed research together up until Pierre Curie's death. Their path was paved by the late-nineteenth century discoveries of Henri Becquerel in the area of x-rays and radioactive properties. One of the Curies' most significant contributions was the isolation of two new radioactive elements—radium and polonium. The nuclear age would rely greatly on these discoveries. The Curies won half of the 1903 Nobel Prize in physics for their work in radiation (Becquerel won the other half of the award that year). Einstein, of course, won the 1921 Nobel Prize in physics for his work on the photoelectric effect, so it is clear that Einstein's and Curie's work were of equal scientific caliber.

Einstein met Marie Curie at the first International Solvay Conference. This meeting was held in 1911 in Belgium, and some of the greatest minds in physics of the time were in attendance. This time was actually a dark period in Marie Curie's life; her rapidly expanding fame led her to become the victim of discrimination because of her gender and alleged religion. Female physicists were definitely not the norm in the early twentieth century. In addition, Curie was officially from a Catholic family but her former last name, Sklodowska, suggested Jewish origins; this apparent discrepancy led to much of the same suspicion that Einstein faced as a Jew.

Marie Curie and Einstein became friends, perhaps sharing the burden society cast upon them, and actually vacationed together with their children in 1913. They shared professional interests and appeared to enjoy each other's company.

Another similarity is that, like Einstein, Marie Curie's work was soon applied to areas outside her direct circle of influence. Einstein's work on the photoelectric effect, for example, allowed the development of the field of quantum mechanics. Curie's work with radiation allowed abstract painters such as Wassily Kandinsky to use the fluidity of decay as a metaphor for their work; x-ray photography would become an art form in and of itself.

The International Solvay Conference of October 1927 presented another opportunity for Curie and Einstein to meet and exchange ideas. This meeting allowed physicists from all over the world to discuss new theories. In addition to Curie and Einstein, those in attendance included Max Planck, Niels Bohr, Werner Heisenberg, Erwin Schrödinger, and many other famous physicists.

While their research was carried out largely independently, Einstein and Curie were defining history and were very much aware of each other's ideas and work. Albert Einstein had great regard for Marie Curie, calling her one of the only people he knew who had not been corrupted by fame.

34. Einstein's response to Schrödinger's equation

In the early 1920s, as Heisenberg was developing his matrix theory of quantum mechanics, other current research resulted in the development of a separate theory of quantum mechanics. This theory, developed by

Louis de Broglie (1892–1987), asserted that the wave-particle duality (which had been accepted for light) could be extended to all matter, particularly electrons. In this theory, the physics of matter and the physics of radiation were finally joined—according to de Broglie, and even solid matter had a wavelength.

Beginning around 1921, Erwin Rudolf Josef Alexander Schrödinger (1887–1961), an Austrian scientist, engaged in studies of the nature of the atom. He worked with quantum statistics in the mid-1920s, and he was aware of Louis de Broglie's work. He entered the University of Vienna in 1906 and studied theoretical physics, such as Maxwell's equations, thermodynamics, optics, and mechanics. He received his doctorate degree in 1910 and, after a brief stint in the military, took a job working in experimental physics. This break from theoretical physics would prove invaluable to his later work because it provided him with a practical backdrop for his research.

Erwin Schrödinger worked this new description of electron matter into a comprehensive wave theory. Schrödinger's wave equation is famous because it relates wave mechanics to general relativity. In fact, Schrödinger created the second formulation of quantum mechanics, called the wave function formulation.

At this point, around 1925, there were two complete, internally consistent theories of quantum mechanics: the wave formulation and the matrix formulation. Fortunately, it was soon proven that the two theories were actually mathematically equivalent to each other, although expressed in different ways.

$\Sigma \theta' \frac{\lambda}{\pi \Delta} \lambda \, ^{\alpha} \frac{\lambda}{\pi \theta}$ $^{\alpha} \pi \, \theta_\Delta \Sigma \theta' \frac{\lambda}{\pi \Delta} \lambda \, ^{\alpha} \frac{\lambda}{\pi \theta} \Delta \frac{\sigma}{\Sigma} \pi \chi \, \Delta^{\alpha} \pi \Sigma \theta \, ^{\alpha}_{\pi \Delta} \lambda \, ^{\alpha} \frac{\lambda}{\pi \theta} \Delta \frac{\sigma}{\Sigma} \pi \chi \, \Delta^{\alpha} \pi \, \theta_\Delta \, ^{\alpha}$

Einstein's response to the new quantum theory seems to have been mixed. On the one hand, he supported the new breakthroughs, while on the other, he was worried by the element of chance that seemed to have entered the orderly, predictable world of physics. In 1924, before the competing versions of quantum mechanics had been reconciled, Einstein bemoaned the fact that there were now not one, but two theories of light, which seemed to have no logical connection with each other. In that same year, Einstein also was resistant to Bohr's solution to the paradox of how the electron can know when to emit radiation.

One of Einstein's fellow scientists, Schrödinger, began conversing with Einstein in the 1920s; the two exchanged letters on the subject of physics and contemporary scientists. While he was initially resistant to quantum theory, when Einstein read Schrödinger's wave mechanics formulation in 1926, Einstein wrote to him, expressing how impressed he was with his work. Einstein stated that it seemed to be the work of pure genius and that Schrödinger's research provided a decisive advance in quantum theory.

By 1926, Schrödinger had published new papers on wave mechanics and was gaining worldwide fame. He won the Nobel Prize in physics in 1933. By the 1940s, Schrödinger was starting to work actively on creating a unified field theory. He published a paper on it in 1943 and, in 1946, Schrödinger corresponded with Einstein on the subject. Although Schrödinger never reached another conclusion of any significance, he would continue this elusive quest for the remainder of his life.

35. How Einstein's work overlapped with the work of Max Planck

Max Planck (1858–1947) was a noted German physicist who challenged many notions of classical physics. He developed a quantum theory of physics, which Einstein used in his own explanations of photoelectricity. The son of a professor of law, Planck earned his doctorate in 1879, and after years of academic accomplishment, he became a full professor at Berlin University in 1889. Research in his early years focused on entropy, thermodynamics, and radiation. Planck won the Nobel Prize for physics in 1918, and in 1930, he was appointed president of the Kaiser Wilhelm Physical Institute.

One of his most important breakthroughs was in the study of what was called "black body radiation," or the radiation emitted by solid bodies once they had been heated. The current physics model of the time couldn't explain his results so, in the true spirit of burgeoning science in the twentieth century, Planck changed the model.

The main puzzle of black body radiation, as considered by Planck, was related to the amount of heat that was given off by a heated body at various wavelengths. He was able to explain the odd experimental results if he assumed that radiation was quantized, and that it could only be given off in certain predetermined amounts. His seminal work in this area was codified by a relationship he developed between the frequency and energy of radiation around 1900. Planck required a multiplier, or a constant value, to make the relationship hold true. He described this relationship in terms of a universal constant, which is commonly called h, or Planck's constant.

Planck will be remembered throughout history for his work in this area. It fundamentally changed the way in which physics was conceived, overturning the views of Maxwell and others who had considered radiation as a continuum process—a process that could take on any arbitrary value. Although his ideas were so radical as to be frighteningly disruptive to the status quo, years of proof would give Planck approval and validity. Einstein would rely greatly on Planck's research for his work on the photoelectric effect, as would Niels Bohr for his research on the structure of the atom.

In fact, Einstein's work and Planck's would overlap on all levels. Planck showed that energy could be quantized, or referred to in terms of discrete units of energy, and that the size of these quanta depended on the frequency (or color) of light. This revelation would prove to be of primary importance in Einstein's work as well. The wave-particle duality would impact both scientists' research, as would further developments in the study of electromagnetic radiation. Planck and Einstein together are commonly attributed with redefining physics in the twentieth century.

On a personal level, Planck (like Einstein) was a pacifist. Although projects relating to war were plentiful during his lifetime, Planck refused to work on any project whose research went directly to the war effort. He adamantly opposed both Hitler and anti–Semitism in general. Planck was personally torn by the influence of the Nazi regime in Germany. He was philosophically against the terror Nazis imposed on the Jews, but he also felt an obligation to remain loyal to his country. He differed substantially in this regard from Einstein and other European scientists of the time.

However, he did share other personal traits with Einstein, such as his love of music.

36. MAJOR INVENTIONS DURING EINSTEIN'S LIFETIME

The first part of the twentieth century was filled with invention and not just in science. Many aspects of modern society were being formed, and the period was ripe with creation and innovation. The twentieth century was a grand time to be an inventor, in no small part because advances in science and technology provided for the existence of innovation in other areas. Some of the major innovations of this period (which would be relevant to everyone at the time, including Einstein) included the automobile, the airplane, the radio, the phonograph, and jazz music.

The history of the automobile is more complicated than one might expect. Contrary to popular belief, Henry Ford didn't invent the automobile. In fact, Renaissance artists such as Leonardo da Vinci came up with designs for motorized vehicles, although such designs would not be executed for hundreds of years. Nicolas Cugnot developed the first steam-powered vehicle in 1769, but the vehicle had to stop to build up power every few minutes, and so it was not very efficient.

The first gas-powered cars came about toward the end of the nineteenth century. In 1885, German engineer Gottlieb Daimler invented the precursor to the modern gasoline engine. Scientific developments led to the refinement of the internal combustion engine, which became the

$\Sigma\theta'\frac{\dot{z}}{\pi\lambda}\,{}^{\circ}\dot{\pi}\theta$ ${}^{\alpha}\pi\,\theta_\Delta\Sigma\theta'\frac{\dot{z}}{\pi\lambda}\,{}^{\alpha}\dot{\pi}\theta_\Delta\frac{\sigma}{2}\pi\,{}^{\chi}\Delta^{\pi}\Sigma\theta\,{}^{\alpha}\frac{}{\pi\lambda}\,{}^{\alpha}\dot{\pi}\theta_\Delta\frac{\sigma}{2}\pi\,{}^{\chi}\Delta^{\pi}\,\theta_\Delta{}^{\alpha}$

primary force behind the creation of the modern motorcar. The first patent for a gasoline-powered automobile was given to Karl Benz, a German mechanical engineer, in 1886. While a variety of ventures produced automobiles one at a time, it was the assembly line that truly allowed for mass production of cars.

Mass production was incredibly important for the automobile to take off as a viable invention for two main reasons. Cars were suddenly available to many more people and increased efficiency in automobile production would bring the cost down considerably, making them accessible financially. The curved dash Oldsmobile was the first car to be mass produced using an assembly line in 1901, although Henry Ford dramatically improved the concept of the assembly line in 1913. Ford's Model T of 1909, while not the first automobile, was one of the first to be mass produced successfully. These innovations in automobile design and production were roughly contemporary with Einstein's development of the theory of special relativity.

The airplane was another seminal invention that would change the way people worked and traveled. Prior to the twentieth century, when people had to travel across the ocean, they had two options: either take a lengthy excursion by boat, or swim. But late-nineteenth-century innovation would lead to the development of an entirely new way to travel—the airplane. The late 1890s was a period in which a number of inventors were trying their hand at developing flying machines. German inventor Otto Lilienthal's hang glider experiments, for example, served as a major predecessor to the airplane.

The first major successful airplane innovation, though, would come at the hands of two Americans, the Wright brothers. Orville and Wilbur

$\Sigma\theta^{\dot{}}_{\pi\lambda}{}^{\alpha}{}^{\sigma}_{\theta}\Delta^{\sigma}_{\pi}{}^{\chi}\Delta^{\pi}\theta_\Delta\Sigma\theta^{\dot{}}_{\pi\lambda}{}^{\alpha}{}^{\sigma}_{\theta}\Delta^{\sigma}_{\pi}{}^{\chi}\Delta^{\pi}\Sigma\theta^{\alpha}_{\pi\lambda}{}^{\alpha}{}^{\sigma}_{\theta}\Delta^{\sigma}_{\pi}{}^{\chi}\Delta^{\pi}\theta_\Delta{}^{\alpha}$

Wright, the developers of the first manned airplane, were actually trained as bicycle builders; they owned a bicycle repair shop before turning to aviation. After years of study and testing, in 1903 they successfully flew their first heavier-than-air craft in Kitty Hawk, North Carolina.

The development of the airplane represented an historical turning point. Not only could people suddenly travel to places that had been previously unreachable, they could do so relatively quickly. Commerce enjoyed entirely new boundaries as well, making it possible to sell goods in places previously unthinkable. The airplane would also have political ramifications; it would change the way wars were fought. The bombing of Hiroshima, for example (in which Einstein had a minimal role) couldn't have been conceived, let alone carried out, if not for the advent of air travel.

Twentieth-century innovation was certainly not limited to automobiles and airplanes. The invention of the radio closely paralleled the technology that made possible other new inventions, such as the telephone and telegraph. James Maxwell actually predicted that the transmission of radio waves would be forthcoming—and how right he was. An Italian inventor named Guglielmo Marconi sent and received the first radio signals in 1895, and the first transatlantic radiotelegraph message was sent in 1902.

Technically speaking, of course, Marconi did not invent the radio wave. What he created was a means to manipulate and transmit radio frequencies. He was not the first person to work with radio waves, either. Michael Faraday (1791–1867) developed a theory of electrical inductance that was actually the beginning of the research that would eventually allow radio waves to be directly manipulated. Heinrich Hertz, a

German physicist, demonstrated electromagnetic waves of energy in 1887. In 1892, French physicist Edouard Branley developed the first electromagnetic wave receiver. Marconi followed this invention in 1895 with the first complete wireless system.

Radio would transform the way people received information. The Russo-Japanese War of 1905 was the first war where news was reported via wireless radio transmissions, and by 1906 weather reports were being sent via radio. News could be transmitted more quickly than ever before, and decisions could be made with unprecedented timeliness. Lines of radio transmission between America and Europe were opened in 1910. Radio would prove to be an especially useful communications tool during World Wars I and II. This new media world, of course, also became very important in propagating news of the latest scientific breakthroughs, including those ideas produced by Einstein and others.

37. THE SCIENTIFIC BACKGROUND OF EINSTEIN'S TIME

The period before Einstein began his work, the mid- to late-1800s, was ripe with scientific invention and discovery. Medicine, mechanics, chemistry, biology, and a range of other fields all benefited from a series of "firsts." What a century of discovery.

Some of the many advances made in the mid-nineteenth century include the first anesthetized surgery in 1846, Englishman Henry Bessemer's 1854 invention of the first process for mass producing steel; and

Charles Darwin's theory of evolution in 1859. The law of chemical equilibrium was established in 1864, the first "modern" telephone was invented around 1877, and photographic film was produced in 1885. By 1895, the first moving picture had been created.

Major scientists, before and during the nineteenth century, were of paramount importance in determining how twentieth-century science would be established. Einstein relied heavily on the advances made by his predecessors. In addition to the other scientists already discussed, research developed by Ernst Mach and Michael Faraday was extremely important for Einstein.

In the nineteenth century, Michael Faraday made some of the most significant advances in the study of electricity. As a child in England, Faraday began experimenting with electricity; he also studied chemistry and other sciences. In 1821, he discovered what would become the field of electromagnetism—the theory of how electricity relates to magnetism. Part of the theory of electromagnetism proved that visible light belonged to a much larger spectrum of electromagnetic (EM) radiation. This spectrum included all types of waves, including radio waves and x-rays.

Faraday built the first electric motor during this period. His device involved a coiled wire, which carried an electrical current, wrapped around a magnetic pole. He was able to produce motion using this scheme. The 1830s marked the period in which Faraday would unveil the means by which electromagnetic induction worked. Electric current could be induced through the motion of a magnet; this new method for generating

$$\Sigma\theta \dot{\pi}^{\dot{\chi}}_{\lambda} \, ^{\alpha\dot{\beta}}_{\theta} \qquad ^{\prime\prime}\pi\,\theta_\Delta\Sigma\theta^\gamma_{\pi\lambda} \, ^{\alpha\dot{\beta}}_{\theta}\mathcal{L}^\sigma_\pi \chi \Delta^\pi \Sigma\theta^{\,\alpha}_{\pi\lambda} \, ^{\alpha\dot{\beta}}_{\theta}\mathcal{L}^\sigma_\pi \chi \Delta^\pi \theta_\Delta^{\,\alpha}$$

electricity would change the way power stations worldwide operated. Faraday's research set the backdrop for James Maxwell, whose work Einstein would later refute.

Another essential contributor to the general state of nineteenth-century science was Ernst Mach (1838-1916). His philosophy and science laid important groundwork in providing Einstein a framework within which relativity could be created. Mach was an Austrian scientist who belonged to the school of positivism, a philosophy that posited the idea that objects could be understood by their sensation as well as their physicality.

This idea impacted Einstein greatly. It implied that time and space were not absolute notions, and in this sense Mach went directly against the prevailing ideas of the time. Mach's rejection of Newtonian concepts of time and space gave a background for Einstein's later suggestion that space and time were not absolute.

Mach also worked extensively in the area of wave dynamics and optics. His early research particularly contributed to the growing field of acoustics. He combined these areas of interest by studying the Doppler effect. This was a concept first solidified in 1845 by Austrian Christian Doppler (1803–1853). It is the idea that, to a stationary observer, waves appear to change in frequency (or wavelength) if they are emitted by something moving. This phenomenon is best explained by the way a train whistle, for example, will appear to change in pitch as the train approaches, then rushes past someone standing still. Mach was always interested in the senses, both in terms of physics and perception. He also studied what would be more futuristic principles, such as supersonic speed.

Another part of Mach's research involved the creation of a theory of inertia. The basic idea behind inertia followed Newtonian principles; bodies at rest tend to stay at rest unless they are acted upon by a discrete force. Mach contributed a different view of inertia in which only relative motion, rather than absolute motion, was important. Einstein would later coin an expression, "Mach's principle," that referred to Mach's idea that the inertia of one body was related to all other bodies in the universe. These ideas came into play in a major way for Einstein and his study of relativity, especially in his development of relative frames of reference with no absolute rest frame.

Part 3

Do you know what $E = mc^2$ really means? No, it is not the theory of relativity. It is the energy to mass conversion formula and is perhaps the most commonly mistaken scientific formula in the world. Not unlike the man himself, Einstein's work may be widely known, but it isn't easily understood.

What made Einstein's work so important is that he took many of the generally accepted theories of the time and expanded them in ways no one had thought of before. At first, some scientists were reluctant to embrace his work, but Einstein persisted, offering more and more evidence to support his work.

From expanding basic principals to physics to his impact on quantum theory (a concept he didn't fully embrace), Einstein's work still amazes scientists and historians alike to this day.

38. EINSTEIN AND THE SCIENTIFIC METHOD

Before examining Einstein's scientific work, his specific theories, and their implications, it is imperative to have a basic understanding of the scientific method itself. Start by thinking of the realm of science as being composed of two main elements: fact and theory. Facts are proven truths that have stood their ground, through the tests of time and the rigors of usage. Facts are things that are taken for granted to be true and unambiguous.

But most facts don't start out as such, particularly in the world of science. In a field where innovation is part of the job, scientists are at times tasked with creating fact from scratch. Such creation does not come easily nor is it handed to scientists on a silver platter. People are inquisitive and, by nature, have a tendency to question the environments and situations surrounding them. Sometimes things that are taken for granted as truth must undergo rigorous examination and must be questioned by many, many people before they are finally accepted as fact.

Enter the theory. What exactly is a theory? It can be generally defined as a set of ideas that relate to each other in some way. Theories differ from facts in that they are unproven ideas; a theory is, by definition, speculative and not certain. Scientists, musicians, artists, philosophers, and people from just about every walk of life create theories every day. How? Simply by observing and thinking about the world around them.

Einstein's ideas were called "theories" because they were initially unproven. They did not start out as facts; they were ideas that had to be tested. This aspect is, in and of itself, unremarkable. Most large-scale ideas that present new concepts, or suggest a reversal of old ideas, are going to be questioned by someone; as such, they will be considered theories until most people agree on their validity. That's the "scientific method"—the method by which science tries to develop more and more accurate descriptions of the natural world around us. The foundation of the scientific method is experimental verification—any idea must be tested before it can be accepted.

The scientific method is the basis of Einstein's work and of all other scientific research—in the past, present, and future. The scientific method begins with a hypothesis, which is a new thought or idea to explain some observation of the world around us. The hypothesis must be testable; this is the main difference between science and other fields such as religion or philosophy. In science, once a new idea or explanation is proposed, it must make specific claims or predictions that can be tested.

The scientific method consists of the following steps:

1. Observation of a particular phenomenon.
2. Formulation of a hypothesis to explain the observations.
3. Use of the hypothesis to make further predictions.
4. Performance of experiments to test the predictions made by the hypothesis.

Then, many independent scientists—not just the one or ones who initially made the hypothesis—test the predictions by performing experiments. If the predictions made by the hypothesis turn out to be correct, then the hypothesis has been proven accurate; it will eventually become elevated in stature to a theory or a law of nature. But even theories can be overturned. For instance, Einstein's theories showed that Newton's laws of classical mechanics, the established theories of the previous century, did not hold up under certain conditions.

So what made Einstein's theories so special? One of the primary reasons Einstein stood out from his predecessors and contemporaries is that the theory of relativity changed the way scientists fundamentally considered both space and time. Humankind's place in the universe was seen from a new perspective, and such a notion was both frightening and exciting. Other scientists had important theories; Einstein's were daring. Sometimes a little excitement goes a long way toward the creation of a legacy.

In fact, Einstein's ideas were so revolutionary that much of the scientific community initially rejected them as being too outlandish. Einstein won the Nobel Prize in physics, but for some much less controversial work he had done early in his career—not for relativity. It took many years for Einstein's ideas to become part of the scientific mainstream.

39. EINSTEIN'S PROOF OF THE PYTHAGOREAN THEOREM

At age eleven, Einstein first read the Pythagorean theorem, and the study of this theorem would eventually influence Einstein's later work. Pythagoras of Samos was a Greek mathematician who lived between 569 and 475 b.c. He is sometimes called the "first mathematician," meaning he was one of the first recorded scientists to have made important contributions to the field of mathematics.

The child of merchants, Pythagoras spent much of his childhood traveling, and he was able to study with famous instructors in Syria and Italy, as well as his native Samos. His early training was in religion, music, astronomy, and mathematics, but was exceptionally interested in math. Pythagoras learned from some of the most capable Greek teachers. He was more than just a mathematician, though—he also studied and worked with religion and philosophy.

Pythagoras was a musician as well; he played the lyre, an instrument bearing notable similarity to the violin. In fact, Pythagoras was one of the first scientists to study acoustics, or the science of the transmission and reflection of sound waves. He used stretched strings to describe sound waves in terms of what would come to be musical terminology. He also created stretched strings with movable bridges, the basis for the modern-day violin, and he showed how the sound would change when the string was plucked at different points along the string. Pythagoras may have even indirectly influenced Einstein's lifelong affinity for the violin in that, from a very young age, Einstein saw the connection between science and music.

Pythagoras' multiple areas of study may have piqued Einstein's interest, since Einstein himself went on to become a student in many different areas.

Pythagoras founded a society whose purpose was to study mathematics; his group was called the Brotherhood of Pythagoreans. Because the organization was largely a secret one, it is difficult to determine precisely which contributions belonged to Pythagoras himself. Composed largely of mathematicians, this school was also devoted to the studies of religion and philosophy. This group may have even inspired Einstein's later formation of his own discussion society. The Brotherhood understood that both the earth and the rest of the cosmos rotated about some angle on a regular basis, and they believed that the movement of the planets might have had a musical logic behind it; Pythagoras' written thesis on this phenomenon was "Music of the Spheres."

Although he pursued many areas of interest, this ancient Greek mathematician's best-known contribution was the Pythagorean theorem, which postulates that the sum of the squares of the sides of a right triangle is equal to the square of the hypotenuse. Although this concept had been known since Chinese and Egyptian times, Pythagoras was one of the first to prove it. The Brotherhood of Pythagoras was also indirectly responsible for proving the existence of both whole and irrational numbers; their model in this analysis was a square whose diagonal could not be reconciled with the lengths of the sides.

$\Sigma\theta^i_{\pi\Delta}\lambda$ $^i{}_\theta$ $^{''}\pi\theta_\Delta\Sigma\theta^i_{\pi\Delta}\lambda$ $^{''}{}_\theta\Delta^\sigma_\Sigma\pi^\chi\Delta^\pi\Sigma\theta$ $^\alpha_{\pi\Delta}\lambda$ $^{''}{}_\theta\Delta^\sigma_\Sigma\pi^\chi\Delta^\pi\theta_\Delta$ $^\alpha$

Einstein became obsessed with the Pythagorean theorem and was able to arrive at a proof after several weeks of work. Pretty amazing for a college student, let alone an eleven-year-old boy. His determination in this endeavor was matched solely by his innate abilities with math and logic.

40. EINSTEIN'S ADAPTATION OF EUCLIDIAN GEOMETRY

Einstein's second formal introduction to mathematics came at age twelve, when he first marveled at Euclidian geometry. Euclid was a mathematician who lived between 325 and 265 b.c., some 250 years after Pythagoras. He wrote a treatise on mathematics called "The Elements," and the fact that this work is still known today suggests that Euclid was one of the Greek world's most famous math teachers.

Euclid's main practical contribution to the field of mathematics came from the basic definitions he created in the course of his work. "Euclidian geometry" is the study or theory of points, lines, and angles that lie on or in a flat surface. It is the simple geometry of lines, planes, polygons, and curves, familiar to any student who has taken a high school geometry course. Such geometry is, in a nutshell, flat. Any elements along a curved surface are considered "non-Euclidian."

"The Elements" both defined mathematical terms and created what have come to be known as the Five Postulates. What is a postulate? It's something that is claimed to be true. In this case, Euclid's postulates can be considered as ground rules for understanding math. The first postulate states that a straight line can be drawn between any two points. The second postulate purports that any straight line can be extended indefinitely. The third postulate says that any straight line can be used as the radius for a circle. The fourth postulate states that all right angles are congruent. The parallel, or fifth, postulate says that for every line and point that is not on that line, there is another, unique, nonintersecting line that passes through that point. Euclidian geometry is in a language of straight (flat) lines, so it satisfies this postulate. While these ideas may seem obvious now, it is important to note that Euclid was, in a way, honest in his thinking and work. He formulated a sound basis for individual, small-scale ideas from which larger postulates and theories would later grow. This aspect of Euclid's stylistic approach to mathematics surely influenced Einstein's later approach to his own work.

What impressed Einstein most about Euclidian geometry was that it was possible to use lines and angles to prove concepts that were not immediately apparent; this aspect of mathematics laid the foundation for Einstein's work. All of a sudden, he understood that it was possible to come up with an idea that had not yet been proven and to create a system whereby that idea could become fact. The same player could create the rules and games; truly innovative scientific thought was possible.

Around 1912, as Einstein was continuing his work on what was becoming known as general relativity, he realized that the simple transformations that had worked in special relativity no longer applied to the more general case. He continued trying to find a more general theory, and eventually concluded that if all accelerated systems are equivalent, via his principle of equivalence (see number 42), principles of Euclidean geometry were not true for all of them. Simple, elegant, and full of geometric and mathematical proofs, Euclidean geometry was just the next vestige of pre-twentieth-century math and physics (following Newton's theories) to fall before Einstein's theory of relativity.

In the new curved space as defined by Einstein, the rules are all different. Parallel lines can meet, triangles can have more or less than 180 degrees, and the universe actually becomes a very weird place. The curvature of space, and space-time, is governed by the distribution of matter and energy. In turn, the curvature of space tells matter how to move. Because space is curved, large, massive objects, such as stars and galaxies, can actually bend and wrap the three-dimensional space around them, much as a rock will stretch and distort a rubber sheet.

41. EINSTEIN'S FIRST EXPOSURE TO SCIENCE: THE MAGNETIC COMPASS

When Einstein was five years old, he came down with an illness that forced him to take bed rest. To help him pass the time, his father brought him a magnetic compass. A compass is a device used to locate magnetic north. Wherever you stand, anywhere on the planet, a magnetic compass will point north. Einstein was fascinated with this interesting device. He would turn it in all directions and, to his amazement, it always pointed in the same direction. This discovery was seminal in his early understanding of physics.

A compass of the sort Einstein had is actually relatively simple in its construction. It consists of a magnet (called the "needle") balanced on a pivot point. Usually the end of the needle is marked with an N, to indicate which direction is north. North is, in fact, not always north. Once every half-million years or so, the Earth's magnetic field reverses direction, and a compass's north end will switch and point south. The location of the magnetic North Pole has also wandered over time, and is not located exactly at the geometric North Pole, which is the rotation axis of the Earth. Still, magnetic north and true north are close enough for compasses to be useful navigating devices everywhere on Earth except extremely close to the poles.

How does a compass work? Imagine that Earth has a gigantic bar magnet inside it, with its south end somewhere around the North Pole. Opposites attract, especially when it comes to magnets, so the north end of the compass needle always points toward the south end of this imaginary bar magnet. All magnets have a north pole and a south pole.

Compasses had been around long before Einstein came along. Greek and Chinese scientists knew about the Earth's magnetic fields, and some of the earliest surviving compasses come from the twelfth century. "Natural magnets" were discovered in the form of ferrites, a type of stone that attracted various metals, including iron. Ferrites were found in large quantities in a part of Greece called Magnesia, and thus the name "magnetite" was given to this mineral. It was later called "lodestone" and was used by some of the first explorers to reach the North Pole.

Magnets today are used for many different applications, and not just for sticking notes to the family refrigerator. They are widely used for navigation and in a range of household appliances, including most headphones, speakers, and telephones. They are used extensively throughout most automobiles.

The compass revolutionized many aspects of society. For the first time, sailors had a tool other than the sun that they could rely on for direction. It has been adapted and improved in modern times and is combined with a gyroscope for more accurate guidance. Some cultures also used the compass to determine the spatial organization of buildings and furniture in an effort to keep man-made space in the perceived proper alignment with nature.

Einstein, being such a curious youth, thought he could somehow trick the compass into pointing somewhere other than north, but he was fascinated by the compass's refusal to play along. Even at this age, he recognized that there was an invisible, untouchable force which guided the universe. This understanding surely influenced the path Einstein would take later in life.

42. ACCELERATION AND GRAVITY: EINSTEIN'S PRINCIPLE OF EQUIVALENCE

Although his 1905 paper on special relativity had brought Einstein, then an obscure patent clerk, no shortage of fame and controversy, he was not willing to let his theory rest as originally proposed. As early as 1907, while preparing a review of special relativity, it occurred to

Einstein that his theory would not fit with Newtonian gravity. He began to wonder how Newtonian gravity would have to be altered to fit with his new theory.

Einstein proposed a thought-experiment, as he had frequently in the past, to consider the problem. In this case, he thought of an observer in a primitive space station—a large chest located far out in space, far enough from everything else that it was not subject to any gravitational forces. Since there is nothing close enough to provide a gravitational attraction, the observer in the chest will float around.

However, Einstein then considered what would happen if a rope were attached to the chest, and some external "being" began to pull on the chest with a constant force. This activity would cause the chest, and the observer inside, to accelerate upward toward the being pulling on the rope. The observer in the chest will no longer float around—he will find himself pulled toward the bottom of the chest and will have to stand there.

The observer can also perform experiments, dropping objects in the chest or rolling them down ramps and will find that they accelerate toward the floor at a constant rate. Thus, the observer will conclude that he is in a gravitational field. If the observer knows that he is in a large chest, he will probably wonder why the chest itself isn't falling, and when he discovers the rope (that the unseen being is using to pull the chest along), the observer will conclude that the chest is, in fact, suspended on the rope.

So, is the observer in the chest just plain wrong? Einstein stated that, in fact, the perspective of the observer in the chest is just as valid as the perspective of an external observer, or one who can see the whole system for what it is. That is, there is no difference between being in a uniformly accelerating chest (reference frame) and being in a uniform gravitational field.

Einstein's principle of equivalence says that there is no way to distinguish between an accelerating reference frame and one in which there is a uniform gravitational field. In other words, acceleration and gravity create exactly the same conditions, and an observer in a closed room cannot perform any experiments to distinguish between them.

This simple thought-experiment leads to the basic tenet of general relativity. Remember that special relativity was based on the idea that all inertial reference frames were equivalent, and that an observer could not tell if she was at rest or in a reference frame moving at a constant velocity. General relativity extends this idea. In general relativity, an accelerating reference frame is equivalent to a reference frame in which there is a uniform gravitational field. This idea is called Einstein's principle of equivalence, and Einstein stated that the discovery of this idea, in 1907, was the happiest thought of his life.

Einstein's principle of equivalence can also work in reverse. Not only can acceleration create what feels like a gravitational field, but it can also cancel out a gravitational field. For example, passengers in an elevator whose cable was cut, a situation in which the elevator would be falling freely toward the ground, would feel no gravitational field—they would be in "free fall." Of course, they would probably have too much to worry about to enjoy the sensation, but the physics of the situation would be equivalent to the observer who was in the chest far out in space, who experienced no gravitational field.

This effect is also similar to what passengers feel in a "free fall" ride at an amusement park, where a car is lifted to the top of a tower, suspended there momentarily, and then allowed to fall to the ground under the acceleration of gravity. During the fall, passengers feel a weightless sensation as they fall at the same rate as their surroundings, although they are strapped into their seats for safety. Of course, amusement park ride designers include a special part of the track near the bottom to decelerate the car and its passengers. Otherwise, they would be in for an unwelcome surprise when they crashed into the ground.

The reason that observers in free-fall experience no gravity is that the acceleration of their fall cancels out the acceleration of gravity. These two forces cancel each other out perfectly only because the masses involved in both cases, the inertial mass and the gravitational mass, are exactly equal. There is no equivalent way to cancel out an electric field, for example, because there is no constant relationship between charge and mass.

43. EINSTEIN AND THE COSMOLOGICAL PRINCIPLE

Soon after publishing his theory of general relativity in its final form in 1915, Einstein began to expand his ideas by looking for applications to other fields. One paper, "Cosmological Considerations on the General Theory of Relativity," published in 1917, single-handedly laid the groundwork for the field of cosmology, which is the study of the universe as a whole. It includes the physics of the universe and the study of the distribution of objects and matter on all scales, as well as their motions throughout the universe. Cosmology is also concerned with the study of the evolution of the universe, including its origin, age, changes over time, and the ultimate fate of the universe.

In his 1917 paper, Einstein used general relativity to model an entire universe. The results of Einstein's initial modeling produced many interesting cosmological elements that are still hot topics in today's study of astrophysics and cosmology, including black holes, the expanding universe, and the beginning (and eventual end) of the universe itself.

In Einstein's 1917 paper, he applied some basic ideas of cosmology to the general theory of relativity, and in the process he expanded the bounds of astronomy as it was currently known.

In the early twentieth century, astronomers were just beginning to understand the large-scale structure of the universe. Our Sun, and the planets orbiting it, make up our solar system. Each star we see in the night sky could have its own planets orbiting it. All these stars—about 100 billion in all—make up our galaxy, which has a spiral shape and is held together by gravity. Our galaxy, and billions of others, make up the universe.

In 1917, when Einstein wrote his first cosmological paper, astronomers had yet to realize that some of the fuzzy patches in the sky were in fact whole separate galaxies, distinct from our own. At the time, it was thought that our galaxy was all there was, and that the fuzzy patches, called "nebulae," were just clouds of gas and dust contained within our own galaxy.

A basic tenet of cosmology is the cosmological principle, which states that the universe is homogeneous and isotropic on the largest scales. This is a critical assumption of the study of the universe as a whole, and it underlies the very study of cosmology itself. There are no special places in the universe, and the universe is the same in all directions—there are no special directions, either.

Beyond this, what does the cosmological principle mean? To understand it, we can break it down into smaller parts. First, homogeneous means "of uniform structure or composition throughout." As applied to the universe as a whole, this clause means that no matter where you are in the universe, the average density of matter will be about the same. According to this principle, the structure of the universe itself is smooth on very large scales, and its matter is basically distributed evenly throughout space.

This clause does not apply on a smaller scale, however. Local regions with more mass than average certainly exist, such as our own solar system's star and planets. Galaxies themselves represent a higher than average distribution of mass. Therefore, on the smaller scale (by the standards of the whole universe), the universe is not a nice smooth distribution of mass but features local enhancements.

The other component of the cosmological principle is that the universe is isotropic. This statement means that the universe looks the same in all directions. There is no one particular direction that an observer can look to see the center of the universe, for example. This means that the universe looks the same to all observers, wherever they are in the universe.

In his 1917 paper, "Cosmological Considerations on the General Theory of Relativity," Einstein took the cosmological principle and applied it to his newly published theory of general relativity. This application resulted in the use of general relativity to model the entire universe, and it was done in conjunction with the Dutch astronomer Willem de Sitter (1872–1934). The results of this work, like so much of Einstein's work, were surprising.

Einstein and other scientists discovered that when the cosmological principle was combined with general relativity, it resulted in a universe that was not static. Instead, the results showed that the universe must be either expanding or contracting. This result was quite momentous, as it went against all the astronomical evidence of the day, which required that the universe be static and unchanging.

44. EINSTEIN'S APPROACH TO A UNIFIED FIELD THEORY

Einstein devoted the last years of his professional career to the unified field theory. The quest began in 1928, but it would occupy his thoughts for years to come. The general definition of a unified field theory is an attempt to create one theoretical framework that describes all the fundamental elements of physics. Such a theory would provide one way to relate everything to everything else, and one method by which all of science would make sense. Does such a thing exist?

It certainly didn't exist at the time of Einstein, and the quest for a unified field theory turned into an all-out obsession for him. He felt strongly enough about the unified field theory to allow it to consume the remainder of his scientific career.

What's so hard about uniting all of physics' fundamental ideas under a single theory? Were these scientific concepts really so incompatible? Unified field theory is sometimes called the "theory of everything"—for good reason. It basically tries to link together all the known methods of explaining science and nature. A "field" is anything that's acting under the influence of a force, like gravity. For example, gravitational fields are what keep us safely on the surface of our planet and what govern the orbits of the planets around the sun.

The formalized idea of a field theory first came about from James Maxwell, in the early nineteenth century. His work in the area of electromagnetism, a specific kind of force, is generally considered to be the first field theory. Much of his research focused on proving that light was actually just a form of electromagnetic radiation. After Maxwell, Einstein's work with general relativity and gravitation would come to be known as the second field theory.

It was Einstein himself who would first coin the term "unified field theory." His quest began with an attempt to prove that electromagnetism and gravity were just different manifestations of the same basic field. Later, his findings were summarized into an effort to bind together the four main forces that scientists believe govern the world. These are electromagnetism, gravity, the "strong force" (the force that holds together the nucleus of an atom), and the "weak force" (the force that deals with nuclear processes such as decay).

Then, however, quantum theory had to be thrown into the mixture. Quantum mechanics is the study of particles, atoms, and other aspects of the universe on a microscopic level. Atoms are studied in terms of subatomic particles such as protons and electrons, and interactions are considered on the smallest possible scale. Relativity, on the other hand, is almost the opposite. It examines the universe macroscopically. Objects are studied on a large scale, certainly large enough to be visible without the aid of microscopes, and they are often viewed with telescopes instead.

The most difficult aspect of Einstein's quest was trying to unite electromagnetism and gravity. The theories describing these two different forces were dissimilar enough that none of his attempts to unite them and bridge the gap between particles and photons made sense.

In his quest for a unified field theory, Einstein did make several predictions that would turn out to be very important in theoretical physics. One such prediction was that energy in the form of both electromagnetic radiation and gravitational energy travels at the speed of light. This very important detail eventually led to the discovery of the weak and strong force fields that accompany nuclear reactions. These forces, combined with the electromagnetic photons they emit, led to Einstein's equivalence of mass and energy, $E = mc^2$. These diverse elements made up several of the major forces that Einstein would ultimately try to unite; however, the existing force field model of the day wouldn't permit a union of the interaction between particles and photons.

Einstein's great disappointment was that he never managed to unite all of physics in one grand scheme. In fact, in his later years, younger scientists believed he had wasted much of his career. They saw Einstein as chasing an unattainable dream while the rest of physics passed him by. However, Einstein never regretted his quest for a "theory of everything." Although uniting all nature's forces still remains an elusive search, Einstein did lay the groundwork for some of today's research on the subject. Some aspects of these different forces have been successfully unified in modern physics. For example, there is a theory called the "standard model." This concept is one that unites the strong force, the weak force, and electromagnetism.

The standard model divides particles into one of two basic types: bosons (the particles that transmit forces) and fermions (ones that comprise matter). Gravitons and photons are examples of bosons, whereas electrons are one type of fermion.

However, this model serves to define only particle physics—only one aspect of what Einstein had hoped to uncover. This description doesn't provide an opening for gravity into the equation. As such, it falls short of ever being a truly unified field theory, because it doesn't take all fields into account.

45. Einstein's first paper of 1905: photoelectric effect

In 1900, Max Planck proposed a solution to the puzzle of black body radiation. He suggested that rather than allowing the oscillating particles in the heated oven to radiate energy continuously, as a wave would, perhaps they were constrained to radiate energy only in discrete packets. He called these packets "quanta." The word quanta (singular quantum) is dervived from the Latin word quantus, meaning "how much." The root is the same for the word quantity, for example. (Contrary to popular usage, a "quantum leap" is actually the smallest possible leap.) According to Planck's theory, the size of the packet of radiation emitted was related to the frequency, so at higher frequencies (shorter wavelengths), energy could only be emitted in large doses.

This theory explained why the energy emitted peaked and then decreased at higher frequencies. Since it could only be emitted in very large chunks at these high frequencies, the probability that any individual particle would have enough energy to emit an entire chunk was very low. Planck found that the size of the energy quantum was linearly related to the frequency: $E = hf$, where h was a new constant now called "Planck's constant." Initially, Planck did not have any justification for his new theory, except that it fit the experimental results perfectly.

Other scientists were also dubious, and Planck's formula was initially disregarded. Not only was there no theoretical justification for the theory, but it also completely contradicted Maxwell's equations of electromagnetism. Energy was not supposed to be quantized; the wave theory of electromagnetic radiation required a smooth continuum of radiation.

Although not many scientists believed Planck's work initially because it had no theoretical basis, Einstein was one of the few scientists to take Planck's work seriously. In 1905, in his first major paper, Einstein suggested a simple and elegant solution to the paradox of the photoelectric effect. Building on Planck's work, Einstein suggested that the photoelectric effect could easily be understood if the incoming radiation absorbed by a metallic surface was quantized.

In this case, rather than being able to absorb any continuous amount of radiation, the radiation would be rationed out to the electrons on the surface in particular doses, or quanta. These quanta had a particular energy that was proportional to the frequency of the radiation: $E = hf$—Planck's relationship, as he had determined in studying black body radiation.

In Einstein's theory, when an electron at the surface of a metal is hit by light, it absorbs one individual quantum of radiation. If there is enough energy to free the electron from the atom it was bound to, the electron is emitted. Unless the electron started out right at the surface of the metal, it must use some of its energy to escape from the metal. Then, once it leaves the surface, it has a kinetic energy equal to whatever is left over of the energy it absorbed from the light.

46. EINSTEIN'S GREATEST BLUNDER: THE COSMOLOGICAL CONSTANT

When developing his theory of relativity, Einstein had to contend with the accepted scientific notions of the universe during his day, which held that the universe was unchanging and static. Astronomers of the day did not observe any general motion in the skies, and thus believed that the universe could not be expanding or contracting. Although his evidence didn't support this idea, Einstein still thought that relativity should support that basic concept, and so Einstein searched for a way to make his theories fit with the observations.

In order to make relativity fit with observations of the time, and keep the universe from expanding, Einstein added an extra term to his equations of general relativity. He found that by introducing a term he called the cosmological constant, he could come up with results that supported a static universe. The Greek letter "lambda" was used to express this term. As with all constants, lambda would have the same value at all points within the universe. This value has sometimes been dubbed the "antigravity term."

The cosmological constant is a term that balances out the attractive force of gravity. It takes the form of a repulsive gravitational force, and it was added as a constant of integration to Einstein's equations. Unlike the rest of general relativity, this new constant was not justified by anything in the current model of gravity—it was introduced purely to achieve the result that at the time was thought to be proper. With the addition of this constant, Einstein's equations described a static universe, fitting the assumptions of the time.

Not everyone thought that the cosmological constant was necessary, however. Dutch astronomer Willem de Sitter (1872–1934), for example, believed in Einstein's initial result, that the universe was, in fact, expanding. He commented that the introduction of the cosmological constant marred the simple elegance of Einstein's original theory, which aside from the cosmological constant, had managed to explain so much without introducing any new hypotheses or constants.

It turns out de Sitter's instincts were right, because Einstein's theories about the cosmological constant did not withstand the test of time. However well-intentioned Einstein was in attempting to maintain the model of the universe as static and nonexpanding, he was wrong. The cosmological constant tried to force the universe into a model that simply wasn't valid, and lambda was seen as shaky not long after Einstein introduced the idea in 1917.

By 1922, a Russian mathematician named Alexander Friedmann was working on creating a model of the universe that didn't require the cosmological constant, and he met with success. He accurately recognized the universe as expanding and came up with a dynamic equation called Friedmann's equation that expressed the changing nature of the cosmos. The Friedmann equation works within the larger framework of general relativity, but it excludes the cosmological constant in an effort to represent the universe as dynamic. Energy conservation is maintained by using the idea that solving this equation for one particle is equal to solving it for all particles.

Later, U.S. astronomer Edwin Hubble provided observational evidence that disproved Einstein's cosmological constant idea. A scientist at the Mount Wilson Observatory in California, Hubble discovered evidence indicating that the universe was, in fact, expanding. He studied the Andromeda galaxy and formulated equations that related a galaxy's velocity to its distance from Earth. Hubble used these equations to deduce that the universe is actually expanding, rather than remaining static.

When Einstein learned of the results of Hubble's work, he realized his mistake in introducing the cosmological constant into his equations. Following the publication of Hubble's 1929 results, Einstein and de Sitter worked to develop a new model of general relativity that could be applied to an expanding universe.

In fact, Einstein had been right in the first place. As it turns out, the cosmological constant that Einstein had introduced to force the universe into stability hadn't been necessary after all. There turned out to be a simple solution to the gravitational field equations in the case of an expanding universe. This idea came to be known as the Einstein–de Sitter model of the universe. In a 1932 paper, Einstein and de Sitter published their results. In this paper, they suggested that there could be large amounts of matter in the universe that had not yet been detected, because this matter did not give off any light. This material has since been dubbed "dark matter," and it has been shown to exist in at least a few situations. Since dark matter cannot be detected directly, its presence has been inferred from the gravitational effects it has on other objects. Dark matter, and the amount of it that may or may not exist in the universe, is a hot topic of study by astrophysicists today.

Einstein officially retracted his version of general relativity that included the cosmological constant in 1932, and he called the cosmological constant the greatest mistake of his career. Even geniuses sometimes make mistakes.

47. EINSTEIN'S SECOND PAPER OF 1905: BROWNIAN MOTION

Brownian motion was first described in an 1828 paper by the British botanist Robert Brown (1773–1858) as the random motion of pollen grains or dust in water. Robert Brown, a gifted botanist, was one of the first Westerners to describe many new species of plants while on a trip to Australia. He was a very skilled observer with a microscope, and he documented the microscopic structure of numerous different plants. He first noticed the odd motion that was called "Brownian movement" (later Brownian motion) when observing grains of pollen suspended in water.

Brown had originally intended to study the minute structure of the grains of pollen, but instead noticed that the tiny particles would not stay still under his microscope lens long enough for him to observe them. Instead, they were in constant motion.

The motion of particles in a liquid can be described as a "random walk." Brown was not easily persuaded that he was watching the motion caused by a living organism. His many studies of various plants led him

$\Sigma\theta'\frac{\dot{z}}{\pi\Delta}\lambda$ $\frac{\alpha\dot{z}}{\pi\theta}$ $\alpha\pi\theta\Delta\Sigma\theta'\frac{\dot{z}}{\pi\Delta}\lambda$ $\frac{\alpha\dot{z}}{\pi\theta}\frac{\sigma}{\Delta}\pi^{\chi}\Delta^{\pi}\Sigma\theta$ $\frac{\alpha}{\pi\Delta}\lambda$ $\frac{\alpha\dot{z}}{\pi\theta}\frac{\sigma}{\Delta}\pi^{\chi}\Delta^{\pi}\theta\Delta^{\alpha}$

to believe that an alternate explanation must be more likely. Brown attempted to see if it was the living essence of the plant pollen that provided the motion. First, he performed observations of plant pollen that had been suspended in an alcohol solution for eleven months. These observations showed the same motion, suggesting that it was not only fresh, living pollen grains that exhibited this behavior.

Brown then attempted to replicate the behavior by suspending fine particles ground from rocks and other inorganic substances. Indeed, particles of rock behaved the same as grains of pollen, exhibiting random motions under a microscope. This behavior ruled out the possibility that some living phenomenon was responsible for the motion.

Having determined that the motion was not caused by some property of living material, Brown was left with a puzzle. He was unable to come up with an explanation for the motion of inert, microscopic particles of material suspended in solution. It wasn't until another of Einstein's groundbreaking 1905 papers was published, seventy-five years later when the mystery was finally solved.

In his second 1905 paper, Einstein used the molecular kinetic view of heat to explain the motions of microscopic particles suspended in a liquid; in other words, Brownian motion. Einstein's explanation was different from other attempts to understand this motion. He showed that it was the movement of tiny molecules, not visible under the microscopes of the day, which resulted in the motion of the larger, microscopic particles.

Einstein's explanation depended on the kinetic theory of gases as studied by Maxwell and Boltzmann. Einstein concluded that the thermal motions of the molecules in a gas caused the tiny molecules to continually collide with the larger particles visible in a microscope. Even though the molecules in a gas (or in water) were not visible themselves under a microscope, their presence could be detected through the study of their effects on the visible, larger particles that they impacted. It was these impacts that caused the continual, random motion of particles that had so puzzled Brown and those after him.

Einstein's approach was important because rather than attempting to use Newtonian mechanics to follow the motion of individual particles, as previous scientists had tried, he instead considered the system as a whole.

Since the velocities of the particles varied tremendously during their journeys, and the paths themselves were incredibly complex, Einstein decided not to base his equations on either. Instead, he defined the displacement as the straight-line distance between the beginning and end points of a path taken by an individual particle. Einstein then observed that the average displacement of particles increased with time. In fact, if the time was increased four times, the average displacement increased two times, and so on. With this line of reasoning, Einstein showed that he could calculate the mean free path for such particles. This path is the average distance that a particle could travel between collisions, as a function of time.

In his work on Brownian motion, Einstein boldly combined ideas that came from very different parts of physics, including kinetic theory, atomic theory, and hydrodynamics. His work also provided a firm theoretical support for the theory that matter consisted of tiny atoms and molecules. He showed that these tiny particles, even though they were invisible, could have an effect that was both observable and worthy of study.

Einstein's work on Brownian motion and kinetic theory spurred French physicist Jean Baptiste Perrin (1870–1942) to perform experiments to confirm Einstein's theoretical predictions. In performing these experiments, Perrin also proved that matter was made up of discontinuous atoms and molecules, and for this work he received the Nobel Prize in 1926.

48. EINSTEIN'S SUPPORT OF BOSE'S THEORY OF PHOTON SPIN

One of Einstein's most famous non-European contemporaries was Satyendra Nath Bose (1894–1974). Bose was a physicist and mathematician from Calcutta, India. His father was an engineer with the East India Railway and appears to have passed on a family interest in science and math. Satyendra Bose taught physics at the Calcutta University and Dacca University and was always engaging in both teaching and research. He was a talented physicist who also studied zoology, chemistry, biology, and anthropology; he is often considered one of the twentieth century's broadest scientific minds.

Bose wrote one of his first articles on Planck's theories while he was working at Dacca University between 1921 and 1945. This paper, entitled "Planck's Law and the Hypothesis of Light Quanta," was rejected by the scholarly organization he'd sent it to for publishing, the *Philosophical Magazine*. Refusing to simply accept defeat, Bose then sent his paper on to Albert Einstein for critique.

$\Sigma\theta^{\chi}_{\pi\lambda}\lambda$ $^{\alpha}_{\pi}\theta_{\Delta}^{\sigma}{}^{\chi}_{\Delta}\pi\theta_{\Delta}\Sigma\theta^{\chi}_{\pi\lambda}\lambda$ $^{\alpha}_{\pi}\theta_{\Delta}^{\sigma}{}^{\chi}_{\Sigma}\pi\chi\Delta\pi\Sigma\theta^{\alpha}_{\pi\lambda}\lambda$ $^{\alpha}_{\pi}\theta_{\Delta}^{\sigma}{}^{\chi}_{\Sigma}\pi\chi\Delta\pi\theta_{\Delta}^{\alpha}$

When Einstein received the paper from Bose, he immediately realized its importance and the need to see it published. In his paper, Bose proposed that photons could exist in different states and that the number of photons was not conserved. This observation led to the property of photons called "spin."

In fact, physicists have now determined that all subatomic properties have an intrinsic angular momentum that is known as "spin." Different classes of particles have different allowed values of spin, and the spin of particles is related to two things: what quantum state the particles can occupy, and how many other particles can also occupy that state.

Einstein was impressed enough to recommend Bose's paper for publication to *Zeitschrift für Physik*, where it was ultimately accepted. Einstein even performed the translation (from English into German), showing the respect he had for Bose's work. This publication was, in many ways, a starting point for Bose's international reputation. He was granted leave from Dacca University and spent time in France; he met and worked with Marie Curie, another of Einstein's associates who was a powerful scientific force. Bose also spent a year in Germany and had the opportunity to work directly with Einstein. In fact, Bose and Einstein later developed Bose–Einstein statistics, which turned out to be a fundamental part of quantum mechanics in determining how one class of particles, called "bosons" after Bose, interact.

Einstein was initially skeptical of the concept of quantum mechanics; he was uncomfortable with the high degree of probability. Bose's paper, though, was a significant factor in Einstein's eventual adoption of quantum physics. He wrote several letters to the scientific community in support of Bose's paper; when he came out in support of something, Einstein was certainly not shy. He voiced his approval and provided solid reasons for supporting Bose. It is likely that Einstein's assistance is one of the reasons Bose is so well known in the scientific community today.

49. EINSTEIN'S THIRD PAPER OF 1905: SPECIAL RELATIVITY

In his third 1905 paper, Einstein proposed a solution to the problem of the speed of light. The first part of Einstein's paper included a new statement of relativity indicating that all the laws of physics are the same for an inertial observer.

Einstein's new statement meant that not only was there no mechanical experiment that an observer could do to prove whether or not she was moving (at a constant velocity), but also there was no electromagnetic or optical experiment that she could do. Einstein stated that the speed of light is the same for all inertial observers, and does not vary or depend on the motion of the source. Observers can't even use the speed of light to tell whether or not they, or the source of the light, are moving.

Einstein's two postulates of special relativity are as follows:

1. The laws of physics are the same for any inertial reference frame.

2. In an inertial reference frame, the speed of light (c) is the same whether it's emitted by a source that's moving (uniform motion, not accelerating) or stationary.

Early views of relativity eradicated the idea of fixed locations in space. An observer in an airplane who walks down a few rows, then returns to her seat, thinks she is going back to the same location in space. However, an observer on the ground viewing the passenger in the moving airplane instead sees her final location as an entirely new place with respect to the ground. This example shows that the two observers do not agree on location—location depends on each person's individual frame of reference.

Einstein's new view of relativity took this one step further. It not only removed the idea of fixed locations in space, but removed the idea of fixed time as well. Events that occur at the same time are simultaneous. Einstein showed that simultaneity is not fixed across reference frames—events that appear to be simultaneous to one observer can occur at different times for a different observer.

These results made time another variable of location in "space-time." With the help of the German mathematician Hermann Minkowski (1864–1909), Einstein showed that events could be thought of as occurring at a particular four-dimensional coordinate: three dimensions for the typical spatial location (such as latitude, longitude, and elevation), plus a fourth dimension for time. And just as the three spatial positions can vary according to the reference frame (as in the airplane example), the fourth dimension, time, can also vary.

In formulating his initial work on relativity, Einstein also showed (almost as a byproduct) that there is no ether. Ether was a nineteenth-century construct, an undetectable medium through which light traveled,

$$\Sigma\theta^\iota\pi^\lambda\lambda \ ^\iota\gamma\theta \qquad ^\iota\pi\theta_\Delta\Sigma\theta^\iota\pi^\lambda\lambda \ ^\iota\gamma\theta_\Delta\Sigma\pi^\chi\Delta^\prime\pi\Sigma\theta^{\ a}\pi^\lambda\lambda \ ^\iota\gamma\theta_\Delta\Sigma\pi^\chi\Delta^\prime\pi\theta_\Delta^{\ a}$$

which also established a basic reference frame for all matter. Since Einstein had shown that there was no measurement that could be taken to show whether an object was moving or at rest (including measuring the speed of light in the reference frame), the idea of a natural resting reference frame, which was not moving, made no sense. It could never be proven that a particular reference frame was at rest with respect to all others.

However, the experiments performed by American physicists Albert Michelson and Edward Morley had attempted to detect the speed of light with respect to the ether, which they assumed was a natural rest frame. If there were such a natural reference frame, then the speed of light would be measured relative to this frame, and it would vary in different reference frames. Since the speed of light is a constant, there is no natural reference frame. The ether cannot exist. The speed of light is a constant as measured with respect to the observer, and if an observer sets up an inertial reference frame and measures the speed of light, she will always find it to be the same value (which we use the symbol c to denote).

So what about the need for an ether as a medium for light to move through? What is doing the "waving"? It turns out that light waves are not compression waves like sound waves; they are transverse waves. This type of wave does not require a medium and can easily travel through space or a vacuum. Thus, electromagnetic radiation, including light, can travel through either air or the vacuum of space without requiring an ether or any other medium to be present.

The removal of the ether from scientists' conception of the universe certainly required hard facts and evidence, but it was also a leap of faith.

Σθ‘⊼λ ‘⁷θ⸹₂π̅ χᐃ̈π θᐃ Σθ‘⊼λ ‘⁷θ⸹₂π̅ χᐃ̈πΣθ ᵘ⊼λ ‘⁷θ⸹₂π̅ χᐃ̈π θᐃ ᵘ

For the first time, the world was considered complete without this mystical medium. Scientists, philosophers, and everyone else would have to grapple with the idea that there was no single medium binding everything together. Questioning the basics would become a fundamental part of early twentieth-century life. This might have made many people uncomfortable, but it also set the stage for the incredible wave of innovation that would follow Einstein's discovery.

In addition to the strange outcome mentioned previously, where events are no longer simultaneous if measured from different reference frames, special relativity also results in some very odd behaviors when velocities approach the speed of light. Exploring some of these strange consequences, which are all consistent with Einstein's view of the universe, led to the many exciting ideas that influenced the path science would take.

One of Einstein's most famous thought-experiments is time dilation. In this case, imagine two clocks, one that is moving with an observer on a train and one that is stationary on the ground. Imagine that these are light clocks, in which time is measured by having a pulse of light bounce from one mirror to another, as detected by a light detector. If the observer on the ground looks at his clock, he will see the light pulse bounce back and forth from one mirror to the other in a straight line, measuring time. Similarly, the observer on the train will see the same thing if she looks at her clock, which is moving on the train with her.

However, suppose that the observer on the ground decides to check the time using the clock that's moving on the train. He watches one pulse of light bounce off one mirror, then bounce off the second. But in the time the light took to travel from one mirror to the other, the whole clock moved some distance down the track on the train. So the path that the light takes from one mirror to the other will look like a zigzag pattern to the observer on the ground.

The observer on the ground can compute the distance traveled by the light pulse, and he knows that the speed at which it is traveling is c, the fixed speed of light. Since speed multiplied by time gives distance, he can see how much time it took the pulse to bounce off the two mirrors. That amount can be used to compare the time on the moving clock to the time on his fixed clock.

But when he compares the two clocks, he is in for a surprise. Even though the two observers carefully synchronized their clocks at the start of the experiment, when the observer on the ground compares the time on his clock to the time on the moving clock, the moving clock is running slower than his stationary clock. This effect is called "time dilation."

Time dilation works for any moving clock, not just a special light clock. (The observers could easily have used the light clocks to set their own watches or other clocks in their reference frames.) It is a consequence of the fixed speed of light. Since the speed of light is the same in all reference frames, when the moving clock is observed by the fixed observer it seems like the light pulses travel a longer distance. Because they travel that distance at the same speed (the fixed speed of light), they therefore must take longer to do it. For this reason, time runs slower in the moving reference frame.

This scenario also applies in reverse. If the observer on the train looks at the clock on the ground, she thinks that she is stationary and the ground is moving backward. So to her, the clock on the ground is the moving clock, and she will measure the same time dilation. To her, the clock on the ground is running slow.

Of course, if the train is moving at a typical train speed of about 50 or 60 miles per hour, the change in time on the moving clock will be very small. However, if the train were able to move at a sizable fraction of the speed of light (remember that the speed of light is 186,300 miles per second, so it would have to be an imaginary rocket-train), then the time dilation effect would be much more sizable. In fact, not only clocks run slow in the moving reference frame—everything does, including the body of the observer on the train. So because of time dilation, she will even age more slowly than the observer on the ground.

The effects of time dilation have been measured experimentally. One such experiment was done by synchronizing two identical clocks and then flying one around the world on an airplane while the other stayed at rest on the ground. When the two clocks were compared after the plane flight, the one that had been in motion on the plane showed that less time had elapsed than the one on the ground. In this scenario general relativity also comes into play, but the effects of special relativity are clearly measurable and fit with the predictions from Einstein's theory.

A related effect of moving versus stationary reference frames is length contraction. Suppose that the train moving over the tracks left marks on the track every second, as measured on the train. If the train were moving at 10 feet per second, then the observer on the train would measure that the marks on the track were located every 10 feet.

However, if the observer on the ground measures the distance between the marks, he will measure something different. To him, the train's clock is running slow. According to his clock, then, the marks were left at intervals greater than one second, and therefore are located at a distance greater than 10 feet apart.

This effect is called "length contraction." Length contraction means that to a moving observer, distances look shorter than they do to a stationary observer. In fact, to a moving observer, all distances seem to get squished up in the direction of motion.

Perhaps the most famous thought-experiment related to special relativity is the so-called twin paradox. Actually, it is not a paradox at all, but a problem that can be explained consistently with the principles of relativity as Einstein defined them.

In this story, consider a pair of twins. One, the sister, sets off in a spaceship for the nearest star, Alpha Centauri, which is four light-years away. When she gets there, she turns around right away and comes back to Earth, where her brother is waiting for her. If her spaceship travels at a speed of 0.6 c (0.6 times the speed of light), then according to her brother on Earth, the trip took 160 months (13⅓ years). However, remember that since she is in motion, her clock appears to run more slowly to her brother on Earth (who is not moving; remember the example of time dilation on the moving train). So to the sister on the spaceship, the total time it took her to get to Alpha Centauri and back was only 128 months (10⅔ years). She has aged two and two-thirds years less than her brother.

However, remember that to the sister in the spaceship, when she looks at her brother back on Earth, it looks to her like the Earth is moving backward away from her at the same speed, 0.6 *c*. So to her, it would seem like her brother's clock is running more slowly, and he should age less over the trip than she.

When her rocket ship arrives back on Earth, the paradox goes, who is older? The answer is that the brother is older. The sister, who traveled in the rocket ship to Alpha Centauri and back, experienced accelerations on her trip to Alpha Centauri—the rocket ship had to accelerate when it left Earth, slow down as it reached the star, turn around, and then re-accelerate on its trip back to Earth and brake when it got back to Earth. Because of this, the sister's reference frame is no longer an inertial reference frame.

50. EINSTEIN'S THOUGHT-EXPERIMENTS

Einstein was a major proponent of the "thought experiment," the idea that by letting the mind wander and explore, a person determines answers to questions that were seemingly unsolvable. The concept of the thought-experiment was certainly not unique to Einstein. Scientists often devised small examples that would prove much larger concepts. Sometimes these examples were theoretical in nature, while other times they were quite practical; because they were often so simple and elegant in nature, scientists are sometimes more famous for their thought experiments than for

$\Sigma \theta^{\chi} \overset{\dot{}}{\pi} \lambda \ ^{\alpha}\overset{\lambda}{\pi} \theta$ $^{\alpha}\pi \theta \Delta \Sigma \theta^{\chi} \overset{\dot{}}{\pi} \lambda \ ^{\alpha}\overset{\lambda}{\pi} \theta \overset{\sigma}{\Delta} \pi^{\chi} \overset{..}{\Delta} \pi \Sigma \theta \overset{\alpha}{\pi} \lambda \ ^{\alpha}\overset{\lambda}{\pi} \theta \overset{\sigma}{\Delta} \pi^{\chi} \overset{..}{\Delta} \pi \theta \Delta$ ^{u}

anything else. One of Einstein's most famous thought experiments is the "relativity train."

Einstein created a solution to help understand how one observer could think that two events were simultaneous, and another observer think they were not. Imagine a train, with an observer on a car in the middle of the train and another observer on the ground. At some particular time, the two observers are directly opposite each other, and synchronize their watches as they wave to each other in passing. Then, two bolts of lightning hit, one leaving marks at the front end of the train and on the ground at that same point, and one leaving marks at the back of the train and at the same point on the ground. The two observers record the events.

The observer on the ground receives the light from both lightning strikes at the same time. He measures the distance between the two marks on the ground, and finds that he was standing exactly halfway between the two points. Since he knows that the speed of light is a constant, he can conclude that the two lightning strikes occurred at the same time, that is, simultaneously, since the light traveled the same distance to him from each mark and the two signals reached him at the same time.

The observer on the train, however, comes to a different conclusion. She is standing in the middle of the train, and so she knows that the distance from the mark left by the lightning at the front of the train is the same as the distance from the mark left by the lightning at the back of the train. However, she receives the light emitted by the lightning strike at the front of the train before the light emitted from the lightning strike at the back of the train. Since she knows the speed of light is a constant, and the distance from each mark is the same, she concludes that the lightning strike at the front of the train happened before the lightning strike at the back of the train.

How is this possible? The two events were simultaneous for the observer on the ground, but they are not simultaneous for the observer on the train. We can understand how this happened by looking at the motion of the observer on the train. During the time that it took for the light to get to her from the front and back of the train, she was moving along with the rest of the train. The direction of her motion was toward the front of the train. So as compared to the distance on the ground, the light from the front of the train had to travel a smaller distance to get to the observer, while light from the back of the train had to travel a greater distance. This difference in travel time explains why the observer on the train concluded that the light from the two events was not simultaneous.

The relative train shows how the fourth dimension, time, can vary depending on the observer.

Thus, Einstein's initial work on relativity showed that neither space nor time is absolute. The perception of each depends on the observer and her reference frame. However, Einstein did replace these notions with a new, more fundamental absolute. In his new theory of space and time, the one absolute was light. The speed of light is absolute, independent of reference frame. So while two observers will never agree on which of them is in motion, or whether events are simultaneous or not, they will both always agree on the speed of light. As odd as this theory sounds, Einstein's new view of relativity actually made a number of predictions that have been tested and found to be true. Einstein's view of the universe seems to be correct.

51. EINSTEIN'S FORMULATION OF AVOGADRO'S NUMBER

The last of Einstein's influential 1905 papers was, in fact, his doctoral dissertation that was submitted for publication in April 1905. This paper was entitled "A New Determination of Molecular Dimensions." This doctoral dissertation was only seventeen pages long. It was originally rejected for being too short, but Einstein added one sentence and resubmitted it, and it was accepted by his thesis advisor and the Eidgenössische Technische Hochschule (ETH). Bigger isn't always better.

In this work, Einstein showed how to calculate the sizes of molecules and Avogadro's number. This turned out to be one of Einstein's papers that have been referenced the most by other scientists over the years. Einstein used some experimental results on the diffusion of sugar dissolved in water to calculate the size of sugar molecules. These results suggested that sugar molecules were only about 1 nanometer in diameter (equivalent to 1 billionth of a meter). Einstein's new results also showed that when sugar was dissolved in water, some of the sugar molecules actually attached themselves to the water molecules. This result was a new one, and it caused the scientific community to take notice.

As part of the research for this paper, Einstein found expressions for the viscosity and the diffusion coefficient for a hard sphere in a continuous medium. Using these expressions and some experimental data based on diluted solutions of sugar in water, he obtained a value for Avogadro's number that was very close to the currently accepted value.

Avogadro's number is defined as the number of molecules in a gram mole of a particular elemental substance. It is named after the chemist Amedeo Avogadro (1776–1856), who first suggested the idea that elements had particular weights; although the term was named in his honor, Avogadro did not actually calculate the value of this number. In fact, the term "Avogadro's number" was first used by Jean Baptiste Perrin in 1909 in his paper that followed Einstein's theoretical result and calculated the size of molecules.

So what is Avogadro's number good for? Avogadro's original theory, in 1811, suggested that a particular volume of any gas, at the same temperature and pressure, contained the same number of molecules no matter what gas it was. Experiments were made, and eventually it was concluded that one cubic centimeter of gas contained Avogadro's number of gas molecules, or about 6×10^{23} molecules. The current value of Avogadro's number is actually 6.022×10^{23}, as determined by experiments using x-ray diffraction. Avogadro's number is very difficult to determine, and many experiments over the years have refined this current value.

Avogadro's number is also used to define the mole. A mole, in addition to being a small furry mammal, is defined in chemistry as the amount of a substance that contains Avogadro's number of molecules (or other units). A mole of oxygen contains 6.022×10^{23} oxygen molecules.

Avogadro's number can also be used to convert between number and mass. Chemists defined the "atomic mass unit (amu)" as a relative measurement of mass. Since atoms and molecules are difficult to see even with the best microscope, it is nearly impossible to measure the mass of an individual atom. So scientists defined the atomic mass unit as 1/12 of the mass of an atom of the element carbon-12.

The atomic weights of elements, in atomic mass units, are used to organize elements sequentially in the periodic table. The atomic mass of carbon-12, for example, is 12 amu, while the atomic mass of oxygen is 16 amu. Due to how atomic masses are defined, then, 12 grams of carbon-12 will contain the same number of atoms as 16 grams of oxygen.

But remember the definition of the mole as 6.022×10^{23} units. A mole of carbon, for example, will contain 6.022×10^{23} atoms of carbon, which will weigh 12 grams. The conversion from moles to grams depends on the molecular mass of the substance in question. To convert from moles to grams, just multiply by the molecular mass in grams per mole.

In coming up with a theoretical way to calculate Avogadro's number, Einstein provided essential support to the atomic theory of matter, which was still in question at the time that Einstein wrote his paper. Einstein's theoretical result spurred Perrin to measure Avogadro's number experimentally, thus providing solid experimental proof for the existence of atoms and molecules.

52. Einstein's Law of Gravitation

After the success of special relativity in uniting space and time, Einstein began working on a more general theory of relativity, which eventually united relativity with gravity. Einstein's work was an extension of the theory of gravity, as originally developed by Galileo and Newton.

Einstein's theory of special relativity revolutionized the way scientists viewed space and time. It combined them into a new theory of space-time in which both time and distance were variable instead of fixed. The only fixed quantity in Einstein's special relativity was the speed of light. However, special relativity was restricted to inertial reference frames—those that did not accelerate or change direction.

Einstein began working almost immediately to generalize his theory of relativity. He wanted a theory that would explain what happened not only in inertial reference frames, but in any frame—moving, accelerating, or changing direction. As it turned out, there was another problem with special relativity: It was incompatible with Newton's law of gravity. In working to unite gravity with relativity, Einstein eventually came up with his theory of general relativity.

Einstein's theory of general relativity can also be called "Einstein's Law of Gravitation," and was based on the work done by Galileo and Newton on gravitational attraction. Starting in 1907, Einstein began his attempts to use gravity as an invariant in a more general theory of relativity, just as the fixed speed of light was the invariable quantity in his theory of special relativity.

One of the problems in generalizing special relativity was that it was incompatible with Newton's law of gravity. According to Newton, if a gravity field is reconfigured, there is an instantaneous response that is felt by all objects affected by the gravitational field as they adjust to the new configuration. However, according to the theory of special relativity, nothing can travel faster than the speed of light—including information. There can be no instantaneous response to changing conditions. Such a response would also require a universal time, another quantity that was inconsistent with special relativity.

To solve these problems, Einstein began work on a new theory of general relativity, one that included gravity as its new invariable quantity. He was first aware of the problem in 1907, soon after the publication of his first paper on special relativity, and began work on the problem in earnest around 1911. His work would finally be completed in the theory of general relativity.

53. THE MATH ERROR, EVEN EINSTEIN COULDN'T FIND

In a rare lapse, Einstein made an error in one of his equations in the 1905 paper on molecular dimensions. It was not until he revised his work five years later that he calculated the correct value of Avogadro's number. Even Einstein didn't always get it right the first time. In fact, Einstein had to get help from one of his students to find the error in his original work.

Einstein's paper on molecular dimensions was originally published as his doctoral dissertation at the Eidgenössische Technische Hochschule (ETH). A supplementary paper was published six months later with improved experimental data. However, in 1911, a scientist named Jacques Bancelin performed a series of experiments and discovered that his results were inconsistent with Einstein's theories.

Bancelin was working in the laboratory of Perrin, who is known for his experimental determination of molecular sizes. Bancelin's experiment confirmed one of Einstein's predictions for a viscosity increase, one that was based on the fraction of the total volume of the liquid that was occupied by particles. The amount of increased viscosity that he measured, though, was inconsistent with Einstein's predictions. Bancelin determined a value of 3.9 for one particular result, while Einstein had predicted a value of 1.

Apparently, Einstein himself attempted to locate the error; his attempts have been kept for posterity in the form of various notes and other markings in a reprint of his paper. He was unable to find the error, however, and wrote to his collaborator and student Ludwig Hopf. Einstein asked Hopf to recheck all the calculations in his initial 1905 paper on molecular dimensions. Hopf was a student of Einstein's from the University of Zurich, where he had enrolled in a physics seminar with Einstein in 1910, as well as attended his lectures on the kinetic theory of heat and on mechanics. Einstein and Hopf also had published two papers together in 1910.

Hopf managed to find a calculation error in some of the derivatives on page twelve of Einstein's dissertation. However, after the correction of the error and updating all formulas and equations that followed it, the value of the result measured by Bancelin became 2.5 in Einstein's prediction, which was closer to Bancelin's experimental value of 3.9 but still quite different.

The correction was published in 1911, and in this paper Einstein redid his calculation of Avogadro's number. The result he got was 6.56×10^{23}, which is very close to the current value as derived from kinetic theory and black-body radiation. Einstein also integrated the correction into the version of his dissertation that was republished in book form in 1922.

Bancelin continued his experiments, eventually arriving at a value for the result in question of 2.9. His result fit fairly closely with Einstein's revised theoretical prediction of 2.5.

54. THE EXPANDING UNIVERSE?

The nature of the universe, whether expanding, contracting, or static, has important implications for the future of our solar system. Within fifteen years of Einstein's publication of his static model of the universe with general relativity, he would be proven wrong. The true nature of the universe was initially revealed due to work by astronomers such as American Edwin Hubble (1889–1953). Beginning in the early 1920s, Hubble and others began to study the nature of the odd fuzzy patches of light that were called nebulae at the time.

Hubble developed a technique to measure how far away objects in the sky were, and he used this technique to reveal that the Andromeda nebula was in fact a hundred thousand times farther away from us than the nearest stars. In fact, Andromeda was a separate galaxy—one that was comparable in size to our own Milky Way, but much farther away. Its great distance is what made it look like a small fuzzy patch of light.

Hubble then measured or estimated the distance to a number of galaxies, showing that many of these nebulae were in fact galaxies in their own right. The Milky Way suddenly became just one of a number of galaxies scattered throughout the universe, rather than the sole location of stars and planets. However, Hubble did not stop with this amazing revelation.

Along with his estimates of galactic distances, Hubble noticed that he could also measure the redshift of galaxies. Objects moving toward us give off light that is shifted in wavelength toward the blue end of the spectrum (blueshifted), and objects moving away from us give off light that is shifted toward the red end of the spectrum (redshifted). Hubble measured the amount that the light from various galaxies was shifted, and he was able to determine that not only were most galaxies redshifted, but that the amount of redshift was correlated with their distance from us. Galaxies that are farther away from us were redshifted more, which corresponds to higher velocities.

Curiously, however, all the shifts were toward the red, meaning that all the galaxies were moving away from us. The only explanation for this phenomenon was if the entire universe were expanding; this expansion would result in everything moving away from everything else as space itself expands. Thus, in 1929, Hubble had provided the first evidence for an expanding universe.

Once the expanding nature of the universe was revealed, the next question was one of origins. If the universe were currently expanding, then at some time in the past all the matter in the universe would have been closer together. Extrapolated back in time far enough, this theory leads to the suggestion that at some finite beginning to the universe, all the matter was located at a single point. Since that time, the universe has been expanding until it is in the state it is today.

This theory is called the Big Bang theory. In it, the entire universe came into existence in a giant explosion, which occurred about 15 billion years ago. During the first few seconds of the existence of the universe, all matter was created—subatomic particles joined together to form simple elements like hydrogen and helium. These gases clumped together, eventually collapsing down under gravity and igniting; they thereby formed the first stars. These stars, during their lifetimes and at the end of their lives in spectacular explosions such as supernovas, created all the heavier elements in the universe.

Since the Big Bang, the entire universe has continued expanding. Galaxies continue to move away from each other, and matter itself gets more and more spread out. But will this type of motion continue forever? Once the expanding universe was established as fact, scientists studying Einstein's equations of general relativity came up with three possibilities for the universe, depending on how much matter it contained.

If the universe exceeded a certain critical density, then eventually the whole universe would collapse back onto itself, in a scenario called a closed universe. If it had less than the critical density, it would keep expanding forever as an open universe. Only if it had exactly the critical density would it be in a balanced, steady-state condition. This final situation is the one that Einstein had believed, and it's why he had introduced the cosmological constant into his equations to keep the universe from expanding. As we have already seen, however, the static-universe theory was disproved.

Although the universe will someday come to an end, it won't be for some time. In the closed universe case, the universe will collapse in a "Big Crunch" about 100 billion years after the Big Bang, or 85 billion years from now. In the open universe, stars will be around for a trillion years. Of course, our sun will burn itself out in about 8 billion years, so we probably won't be around to worry about the end of the universe.

55. Gravitational redshift

Another result of Einstein's principle of equivalence, as discussed in his 1911 paper, is the gravitational redshift. Redshift refers to the fact that when light escapes from a very high-mass body, it loses some energy in doing so, and thus its wavelength is shifted toward the redder, longer wavelength, lower energy end of the spectrum. For this reason, this result is called a "redshift."

Redshifts, and accompanying blueshifts, are common in astronomy when the light from stars moving either toward us or away from us is studied. These phenomena are similar to the Doppler effect, which refers to sound waves. In the Doppler effect, if a police car is standing still with respect to an observer, its siren will consist of a sound at a particular frequency (or wavelength). If the police car is moving toward us, however, in the time in between cycles (or waves) of the sound, the police car will have moved toward us a bit. This motion of the police car causes the sound waves to bunch up; this bunching effectively shortens the wavelength, increasing the frequency and resulting in a higher pitched siren.

Once the police car passes us by, however, in the time in between subsequent cycles or waves, the police car will have moved away from us a bit. The time between waves will be stretched out and the wavelength of the sound will be increased, thereby lowering the frequency and resulting in a lower pitched siren.

Redshifts in light are similar to Doppler shifts. If an object giving off light at a certain wavelength (or color) is moving toward us, the motion of the light source will cause the distance between subsequent wave crests to shorten. The apparent wavelength is shortened, resulting in light that has been moved toward the blue end of the spectrum. This shifted light is called a blueshift. A redshift is the opposite. A source moving away from us will appear to stretch out its light, moving it toward longer wavelengths at the red end of the spectrum, hence the name redshift.

We can see why the gravitational redshift takes place if we return to the thought-experiment performed with a laser in a free-falling elevator on Earth. Instead of shining the laser beam directly across the elevator, however, we shine it from the ceiling down onto the floor of the elevator. Einstein's equivalence principle once again states that conditions inside the falling elevator are the same as in an inertial frame, so the frequency of the light as measured by an observer on the floor of the elevator will be the same as that measured at the source laser on the ceiling.

However, now consider an outside observer who tries to measure the frequency of the light. If the light pulse were sent at the same moment that the elevator started falling, then the observer outside the elevator would measure the same initial frequency as the observer inside the elevator. Since the elevator is accelerating down toward the surface of the Earth, the outside observer will measure the frequency of the light when it reaches the bottom of the elevator as having increased. Thus, light shining downward in a gravitational field increases in frequency (and, therefore, is blueshifted). We could also do the experiment backward, with a laser on the floor of the elevator shining light onto the ceiling. In this case, the frequency of the light would decrease. Thus, light shining upward in a gravitational field decreases in frequency (and is redshifted).

Einstein's prediction was yet again confirmed by observation. Astronomers measured the characteristic wavelengths emitted by certain elements at the surfaces of massive stars and compared them to the results from elements in a laboratory on Earth. Just as predicted, the results from the stars showed a redshift by the expected amount.

56. The history of $E = mc^2$

Along with his three major papers in 1905, Einstein also published a brief paper that described an important consequence of his work on special relativity. This paper described the equivalence of mass and energy. Einstein realized that his understanding of special relativity had many consequences. It not only affected dynamics, the study of moving bodies and their interactions, but it required him to re-evaluate the Newtonian ideas of momentum, work, and energy. In order to understand these consequences, one must first consider a few definitions for momentum, work, and energy.

Momentum

Momentum was first described by the French philosopher René Descartes (1596–1650). Momentum means "amount of motion," and is defined as the mass of a body multiplied by its velocity. A large body moving slowly can have as much momentum as a small body moving quickly. Momentum can be transferred from one object to another—think of a moving billiard ball bumping into a stationary one. If they hit directly, the first ball will stop, and the second will move off at about the same speed. Thus the total amount of momentum, or net motion, stays the same.

While Descartes deduced that momentum should be conserved, it was Newton who formalized the conservation of momentum as part of his laws of motion.

Work

The physics definition of work means that a force has been exerted to move a particular object over some distance. Work is defined as force multiplied by distance, where the distance counts only in the direction of the force. Since gravity pulls all objects downward on the surface of the Earth, picking up an object off the floor involves work. A force is defined as mass multiplied by acceleration, where acceleration is the change in velocity of an object. From this relationship comes Newton's famous equation, $F = ma$, where F is a force, m is a mass, and a is the acceleration.

Energy

The definition of energy is "the ability to do work." There are different types of energy: Kinetic energy is the energy that comes from motion, while potential energy is the energy that comes from position.

The kinetic energy of an object is related to the mass of an object and the velocity at which it is traveling. An object with more mass, or traveling at a higher velocity, will have more kinetic energy than a slower or lighter object. The actual relationship between kinetic energy, mass, and velocity can be expressed as $E = \frac{1}{2}mv^2$, where E is kinetic energy, m is the mass of the object, and v is its velocity.

The simple relationships of Newtonian mechanics, however, become much more complicated when special relativity is taken into account. For objects moving at speeds close to the speed of light, both time dilation and length contraction become important, and it appears that momentum is no longer conserved.

Einstein was worried by this seemingly inconsistent result, and once again he found a simple and elegant way to avoid it. Also as usual for Einstein's solutions, the simple and elegant solution went against almost everyone's common sense and intuition, but was found to be correct based on future experimental results.

In this case, Einstein proposed that the way to ensure the conservation of momentum was to make the mass of an object dependent on its velocity.

As odd as it may sound for an object's mass to increase if its velocity increases, it was confirmed by experiments soon after Einstein proposed it. As early as 1908, a measurement was made of the mass of electrons moving quickly in a vacuum tube, and it was found that their masses were increased by the expected amount.

If you take the kinetic energy of a particle as related to the particle's mass and its velocity in the equation $E = \frac{1}{2}mv^2$, this model works just fine for particles moving at slow, everyday speeds, but things become a bit strange when the speeds approach the speed of light. At speeds close to the speed of light, as energy is increased slightly, the mass increases along with the increase in velocity.

When speeds get very near the speed of light, they can't increase any more. Once particles hit this point, any increase in energy goes directly to an increase in mass of the particle. If we have a particle moving at a speed close to the speed of light, and we apply a force to it for a time interval of one second, the energy and therefore the mass of the particle will increase slightly, by an amount we can call m. Since the force is equal to the rate of change of mass, multiplied by the velocity, this gives us the equation

$\Sigma\theta'_{\pi\lambda}$ ${}^{\alpha}_{\pi}\theta\Delta^{\sigma}_{\pi}$ ${}^{\chi}\Delta^{\pi}\theta\Delta\Sigma\theta'_{\pi\lambda}$ ${}^{\alpha}_{\pi}\theta\Delta^{\sigma}_{\pi}$ ${}^{\chi}\Delta^{\pi}\Sigma\theta{}^{\alpha}_{\pi\lambda}$ ${}^{\alpha}_{\pi}\theta\Delta^{\sigma}_{\pi}$ ${}^{\chi}\Delta^{\pi}\theta\Delta{}^{\alpha}$

$F = mc$ (where F is the force, m is the slight increase in mass, and c is the speed of light, as usual).

So what is the increase in kinetic energy of the particle as a result of applying this force for one second? Remember that energy is the ability to do work, so the increase in energy is the work done during one second. The work done by the force is equal to the force multiplied by the distance. If the particle is traveling at the speed of light c, 186,300 miles per second, then in one second the particle travels 186,300 miles, or c miles. Therefore, the increase in kinetic energy of the particle is equal to the force multiplied by c miles.

So what is the end result? $F = mc$, and $E = Fc$. So we can combine them to show that $E = mc \star c = mc^2$. Does this look familiar? Through deliberate examination of his discoveries concerning special relativity, Einstein was about to compare the increase in the mass of a particle moving at a speed close to the speed of light with its increase in kinetic energy. Thus, the most famous scientific formula was born.

Although $E = mc^2$ explains how particles moving at speeds close to the speed of light increase in mass as compared to their resting masses, what about particles moving at more mundane, everyday speeds? It turns out that mass increases also take place for particles moving at much slower speeds. In fact, over the whole span of speeds from very slow to near the speed of light, particles experience a mass increase that's related to their increase in kinetic energy by the equation $E = mc^2$.

So why don't we notice this effect in our everyday life? Does your mass increase when you are running as opposed to when you are standing still? Even though it may feel like it does, the increase, while real, is so tiny it is very difficult to measure. This is true even at speeds that are significant but still much less than the speed of light. For example, the mass increase of a typical airplane flying at 2,000 miles per hour would only be about half a milligram as compared to its mass while at rest on the ground. This amount is almost undetectable.

57. LAYING THE GROUNDWORK FOR QUANTUM THEORY

Quantum theory, or quantum mechanics, is the study of the behavior of the smallest pieces of matter. It involves interactions on a very small scale— at the level of molecules, atoms, and subatomic particles. For all the incredible breakthroughs that Einstein was able to help bring about through his research and experimentation, much of his most important contribution to quantum theory comes from his attempts to disprove it. To understand why Einstein questioned quantum theory so strongly, you must first understand where it stems from.

Quantum theory is mostly interested in the absorption and emission of energy at tiny scales. In a way, quantum theory is similar to relativity in that it extends the everyday physics of our world to an extreme. In the case of relativity, the classical laws of physics break down at speeds close to the speed of light, for very massive objects. For quantum theory, the classical laws of physics break down at very small scales.

In classical physics, as studied by Newton and others before the twentieth century, energy is considered to be continuous. Matter consists of discrete, physical entities with a specific size, location, and motion. In quantum physics, this orderly pattern breaks down into a confusing, statistical world. Energy is quantized, and is only available in tiny, discrete packets rather than at any possible amount in the continuum theory. These quanta sometimes act like individual particles, but they sometimes act like waves, depending on the situation in which they are measured.

Quantum theory was originally proposed to explain a number of inexplicable results from classical physics. For example, classical physics proposed that electrons orbited around the nucleus of an atom. However, if they orbited in the same way that the planets orbited the sun, the prediction from classical physics was that this system would be incredibly unstable, resulting in electrons spiraling in to the nucleus of the atom in just a fraction of a second. Clearly, however, if this were the case, matter itself would be unstable. However, classical physics was unable to propose an alternate way for atoms to be organized.

The theory of quantum mechanics began with the first realizations that energy levels at a subatomic scale seemed to be quantized rather than continuous, including Einstein's seminal 1905 work on the photoelectric effect. Einstein explained a situation relating to the amount and color of radiation given off from a metallic surface that was exposed to light. The odd results, which were measured experimentally, could be explained if the radiation absorbed by the surface of a metal (as well as the radiation given off) were constrained to certain amounts of energy, rather than having continuous possible energy values.

The study of quantum theory took an important step forward with the discovery of atomic structure. This work began in 1911 with the discovery by Ernest Rutherford (1871–1937) of the atomic nucleus. At that time, the atom was thought of as a mixture, with about the same density throughout its volume, and with electrons scattered throughout, like nuts in a brownie. The negatively charged electron, in fact, had only recently been discovered in 1897 by J. J. Thomson.

Rutherford was conducting an experiment in which he shot alpha particles, which come from the radioactive element radium, at a very thin sheet of gold foil. A beam of alpha particles was at the time called an alpha ray (to distinguish it from higher-energy rays such as X rays and gamma rays). Alpha particles are now known to actually consist of two protons and two neutrons. They therefore have the same form as a helium nucleus. At the time Rutherford was conducting these experiments, however, they were just thought of as another mysterious form of radiation.

In Rutherford's experiment, he tracked the path taken by the alpha particles as they passed through the very thin sheet of gold foil. Most of them just passed right through the foil, which is what he had expected. However, occasionally, one of the alpha particles would instead bounce back off the foil, just as if it had hit something solid. Rutherford was intrigued by this result, and he investigated it very carefully. Eventually, Rutherford was able to trace back the paths of many particles that had bounced back rather than traveling through the foil, and from these paths he could tell that there seemed to be a central concentration of mass in the middle of each atom.

In 1912, Niels Bohr (1885–1962), a newly minted Ph.D., expanded Rutherford's work to include quantum effects. Bohr's research built upon the work done by Planck on quantum theory. Bohr used this body of knowledge to explain why most atoms were much more stable than would be predicted by classical mechanics. First, in studying atoms, Bohr found that when the energy of an electron and the frequency of its orbit around the atomic nucleus were compared, their ratio was equal to Planck's constant. This revelation was Bohr's first clue that quantum effects would be important in the study of atomic structure.

Bohr's most exciting suggestion, however, was in his description of how electrons moved between different energy levels in the outer structure of an atom. It was known that electrons could exist in different energy levels, thought of as orbits with different energies. Orbits that were further out from the nucleus were less tightly bound to the nucleus, and thus energy was required to move an electron from an inner, tightly bound orbit to an outer, less-bound orbit.

Bohr suggested that rather than gradually moving out in distance from the nucleus, electrons instead made quantum jumps from one fixed energy level to another. The odd thing about these jumps was that the electrons never existed in an intermediate energy state at all—they just jumped directly from a higher to lower, or lower to higher, energy level. These jumps corresponded with the atom either absorbing energy or giving off energy. So, if an electron jumps from a higher to a lower energy state, energy is given off in the form of heat or light from the atom, and if an electron jumps from a lower to a higher energy state, that energy must come from the absorption of either heat or light.

It was known at the time that all elements gave off a particular spectral signature, both absorbing light at a variety of very specific wavelengths and also emitting light at very specific wavelengths. Bohr's theory for hydrogen predicted the amounts of energy absorbed and emitted by electrons in a hydrogen atom as they jumped up and down between energy levels, and these values matched the observed spectrum quite well.

Bohr's theory also proved important in understanding the structure of the periodic table. The familiar table of elements that graces every high school chemistry classroom has a very particular structure to it, with elements organized into groups based on various shared properties. Bohr's atomic structure helped scientists understand how these properties are shared between materials with very different masses.

In Bohr's theory, electrons orbited the nucleus in very particular orbits called "shells." Shells of different energies all have different properties, and they can hold only a particular number of electrons before they are full. Once a shell is full, electrons are forced to go to a different energy level. The first shell can only hold two electrons, the second up to eight, the third ten, and so on in a complicated pattern.

It turns out that the outer shell is the most important in terms of how a particular element interacts with other elements, since the outer shell is the most readily accessible (and since inner shells are filled first, the outer shell is the one that's most likely to have any vacancies). Atoms whose outer shells are completely full are very stable, and these are called noble gases. These include helium, neon, and argon. Elements whose outer shells are not completely full tend to be much more reactive. Thus, elements with the same number of electrons in their outer shells are aligned in the same column in the periodic table, and it is this shared position that shows their similar properties.

58. WHY EINSTEIN DIDN'T BELIEVE IN QUANTUM MECHANICS

One of the reasons that Einstein disagreed with the early theories of quantum mechanics had to do with Heisenberg's uncertainty principle. Werner Heisenberg (1901–1976) was one of the primary physicists responsible for defining quantum mechanics. As such, his contribution to the creation of modern physics was enormous, because he laid the foundation for one of its four corners. Heisenberg's research focused on developing the "uncertainty principle" of quantum theory.

The groundwork for quantum theory was laid when Bohr's theory of the quantum energy levels of atoms was expanded by Arnold Sommerfeld (1868–1951) in 1916. Sommerfeld's work included elliptical orbits of the electrons—rather than just the circular orbits in Bohr's initial model—as well as relativistic effects. Bohr, Sommerfeld, and others attracted an array of young, bright students, and they organized a number of centers of study that focused on extending quantum theory to other elements in addition to hydrogen. These attempts, which initially seemed so promising, eventually were unsuccessful.

The main problem was that the "old quantum theory," as it is now called, assumed that the mechanics of a dynamic system (such as electrons orbiting a nucleus) were basically classical dynamics with some quantum effects tossed into the mixture. These theories assumed circular or elliptical orbits just like the ones previous physicists had determined for the motion of the planets around the sun.

It turned out that this treatment worked very well for a simple atom like hydrogen, which has only a single electron orbiting a proton in the nucleus. However, the treatment breaks down once there are more electrons orbiting the nucleus, or one electron orbiting multiple nuclear particles. It became increasingly clear that the so-called "old quantum theory," which was still based on classical effects, failed with respect to any elements more complicated than hydrogen. At this point, various physicists began to try to find a theory to replace it. Two important figures in this search were Max Born (1882–1970) and his assistant Werner Heisenberg (1901–1976).

As a new Ph.D., Heisenberg tackled the problem of trying to determine the allowable quantum states of a particular system. After much tedious work, he eventually reached a breakthrough in determining how to describe the quantum state of a system using matrix algebra, which was a very new mathematical field at the time. In fact, it was Born who recognized Heisenberg's work as part of matrix theory.

Heisenberg's new theory, called "matrix mechanics" or "the matrix formulation of quantum mechanics" turned out to be a very complicated

$\Sigma \theta^c \dot{\pi} \lambda \ \ ^\sigma \dot{\theta} \Delta^{\sigma}_{\Sigma} \dot{\pi} \ ^\chi \dot{\Delta}^{\pi} \theta_\Delta \Sigma \theta^c \dot{\pi} \lambda \ \ ^\sigma \dot{\theta} \Delta^{\sigma}_{\Sigma} \dot{\pi} \ ^\chi \dot{\Delta}^{\pi} \Sigma \theta \ ^u_{\dot{\pi}} \lambda \ \ ^\sigma \dot{\theta} \Delta^{\sigma}_{\Sigma} \dot{\pi} \ ^\chi \dot{\Delta}^{\pi} \theta_\Delta \ ^u$

and unwieldy mathematical description of quantum theory. It was based on the mathematical construct called a "matrix," which is a two-dimensional array of numbers with particular mathematical properties. Despite its complexity, however, Heisenberg's theory was the first complete description of quantum mechanics.

Part of Heisenberg's new formulation of quantum mechanics was his so-called "Uncertainty Principle." As stated in 1927, Heisenberg's principle basically says that the more precisely the position of a subatomic particle is known, the less precisely its momentum can be measured, and vice versa. In other words, if an observer can measure the position of a particle with great accuracy, the particle's momentum cannot be measured nearly as well. But if the momentum is measured extremely accurately, then it will be the particle's position that is comparatively unknown. This idea forms the basis for many aspects of quantum theory.

This Uncertainty Principle has a number of strange consequences, especially those related to causality. In Heisenberg's new indeterminate world, precise knowledge of the present circumstances no longer allowed an observer to predict the future exactly. This result was in opposition to the classical, Newtonian world of physics where if the current conditions of a system, such as a particle's position and velocity, were exactly known, the position of the particle at any future time could be predicted exactly.

As a consequence of the uncertainty principle, probability entered into much of quantum physics, particularly when it came to the orbits of electrons around a nucleus. Initially, electrons were pictured as solid particles orbiting like planets around a sun. But the early attempts at quantum theory and the study of electron waves had revised the orbital picture by representing electron density in various locations around a nucleus. Now, with Heisenberg's probabilistic interpretation, these positions became merely probabilities instead. Physicists subsequently showed atomic structure with probability density plots, providing locations around a nucleus where an electron was more or less likely to be found.

Heisenberg, working with Bohr, continued to formulate quantum mechanics in 1927. Their work resulted in many strange conclusions, including the complementary wave and particle descriptions. In this formulation, any object can be either a wave or a particle until the observer, in the act of observing it, seals its fate by considering it to be one or the other. The wave function that describes the object is, in fact, a combination of both the wave and particle pictures until the act of observation takes place. Thus, in making an observation, the observer actually changes the state of the system she was observing. With these and other observations, Bohr and Heisenberg produced a complete picture of quantum mechanics called the "Copenhagen Interpretation," which they presented at the end of 1927.

Heisenberg's uncertainty principle would later be paraphrased into the notion of the "probability field," the idea that particles had a tendency to exist at certain places in the space-time continuum, although the exact position of any single particle was impossible to determine. Probability was seen as a potentially unifying factor of all the forces of nature. It couldn't be created or destroyed, and its total amount held constant. While this idea never gained universal recognition or proof, it fed into Einstein's idea that such a universal binder might exist.

Einstein initially was very skeptical of the new influence of probability on quantum theory, and was particularly resistant to the idea that the act of observing a system actually changed that system. In fact, he had a series of debates with Niels Bohr on this subject. Eventually, however, he came to accept the mathematical beauty of the probabilistic interpretations.

59. THE CURVATURE OF SPACE–TIME

Einstein's work on general relativity laid the groundwork for the modern understanding of the origin, and ultimate fate, of our universe in the Big Bang theory. It also predicted a number of odd facets of astronomy, including the bending of light by stars. General relativity also suggests the existence of dark matter, a virtually undetectable substance that could fill up much of the universe.

On November 25, 1915, after a number of false starts and other errors, Einstein submitted a paper, entitled "The Field Equations of Gravitation," that finally had the correct field equations for general relativity. Most of Einstein's colleagues of the day were confused and baffled by the quick series of papers between 1912 and 1915, each of which corrected, changed, and extended the previous ones.

In March 1916, Einstein wrote an article that summarized and explained the underpinnings of general relativity in more understandable terms. This article and one he wrote slightly later became the canonical source for general relativity, and both are still widely cited and referred to.

The three main statements of general relativity are as follows:

    1. Space and time are not rigid. Their form and structure is influenced by matter and energy.

    2. Matter and energy determine how space, and space-time, curve.

    3. Space and its curvature determine how matter moves.

General relativity, then, was firmly established in the realm of physics, much to the chagrin of many of the scientists of the day who were resistant to Einstein's new ideas. The theory would prove sound, however, and over the following years as Einstein's fame grew, more and more scientists began to understand and expand on Einstein's groundbreaking theories.

In addition to these results, general relativity also predicts an even more exotic astrophysical object, the black hole. General relativity defines gravity as a curvature of space-time that is caused by the mere presence of matter. The more massive or compact an object, the stronger its gravitational field. The densest, most compact objects in the universe are black holes, which have a gravitational field that is so strong that not even light can escape.

Black holes are just that—holes from which there is no exit because their gravity is so powerful. No radiation at all is given off by black holes, since nothing can radiate away from one without being trapped by its gravity. Black holes can only be detected by indirect means, through their effects on other objects. A black hole can be seen as the end stage of the curvature of space-time—the place where space is so curved that once something enters, it can never get out.

Riemannian geometry gives more clues as to how to understand the curvature of space-time. Georg Riemann (1826–1866) was a German mathematician who focused on understanding how mathematical functions worked. He was one of the first to work on a series of rules to explain non-Euclidian geometry. Riemannian geometry (also called elliptical geometry) does not rely on parallel lines to create form, and says that all straight lines are equal in length. Einstein was particularly intrigued by Riemann's geometry because he decreed the sum of the angles of a triangle to be greater than 180 degrees, which allowed all longitudinal lines to cross at both the North and South poles. There were no true parallels in this theory and, by extrapolation, space must be curved if one considered the presence of circular black holes in the atmosphere.

60. THE PERIHELION OF MERCURY

Einstein continued to expand the theory of relativity, developing much of the mathematics required to describe it along the way (much as Newton had to develop calculus to describe his laws of motion). Einstein wrote a number of papers in 1913 and 1914 in which he expanded the field of tensor calculus and differential geometry, often in collaboration with the greatest mathematical minds of his day.

In November 1915, Einstein made a breakthrough when he produced a solution to the gravitational field equations for general relativity. At this time, he also solved another problem that previously had puzzled physicists and astronomers, related to the advance of the perihelion of the planet Mercury.

And what is a perihelion, you ask? When planets are at different points in their orbit, they will naturally come close to some things (and further away from other things). Perihelion is defined as the point along a planet's orbit where it is closest to the Sun. The opposite of perihelion is aphelion, the point in a planet's (or comet's) orbit where is it furthest away from the Sun. The French astronomer Urbain Jean Joseph Leverrier (1811–1877) was one of the first scientists to perform dedicated studies of Mercury's perihelion. Leverrier taught at the École Polytechnique in 1837 and spent many years at the Paris Observatory. One of his first claims to fame was calculating Neptune's position.

Leverrier first noticed in 1855 that the perihelion of Mercury advanced more per century than could be explained by the theories of the day. The theories of Newton predicted how much the perihelion should advance, but the actual measurement was greater than this prediction. Leverrier spent many years searching for moons of Mercury, which could have explained the effect, but he was ultimately unsuccessful. Other theories were proposed, including changes in the shape or density of the inner planets, an extra planet inside the orbit of Mercury, or a breakdown of Newton's inverse square law theory of gravity. None of these theories was borne out by observation. It was not until many years later, in 1915, that the effect was explained.

In 1915, Einstein took a new set of accurate observations of Mercury, which showed that its perihelion advanced by 43 arc-seconds per century, and applied the theory of gravitation from general relativity. Lo and behold, the theory exactly predicted the measured 43 arc-second advance, without the need to appeal to an unseen planet or satellite or other mechanism.

61. TIME TRAVEL

The concept of time travel didn't originate with Einstein. Ancient Greek philosophers and scientists were keenly interested in the idea of transcending one's physical place in time, and ancient mystics were intrigued with the possibility of interrupting the flow of time. Time is something that

$\Sigma \theta^{\prime} \vec{\pi} \lambda$ $^{\prime\prime}\vec{7\theta}$ $^{\prime\prime}\pi \theta_\Delta \Sigma \theta^{\prime} \vec{\pi} \lambda$ $^{\prime\prime}\vec{7\theta} \underset{\Sigma}{\sigma} \pi \chi \vec{\Delta} \pi \Sigma \theta \overset{a}{\vec{\pi} \lambda}$ $^{\prime\prime}\vec{7\theta} \underset{\Sigma}{\sigma} \pi \chi \vec{\Delta} \pi \theta_\Delta$ ^{a}

everyone understands; you can be late for dinner, early for class, and on time for the train. From time machines to Rip Van Winkle, creative minds in a variety of fields have wanted to explore the manipulation of time as a flexible, fluid element.

There is a common assumption that time is unidirectional; under this assumption, time travel would be impossible. We like to think that time is linear—moving from second to second, minute to minute. To think otherwise throws into question the very essence of our daily routines, our lifestyles, our mortality. However, Einstein wasn't known for maintaining the status quo, and his understanding of special relativity defied these assumptions.

One of the major consequences of special relativity was the notion of time dilation. In a nutshell, the theory here goes as follows: since the speed of light is a constant, the amount of time it takes for someone to get somewhere (assuming "someone" is traveling close to the speed of light) varies depending on if the person is traveling, or observing. The nature of special relativity, then, produces one of the most profound ideas in all mankind: traveling through time is not impossible. Meaning, conversely, that time travel could, in fact, be possible. There is nothing in special relativity to rule it out, and Einstein's theories left room for later theorists to come in and further develop the notion of time travel.

Of course, special relativity only allows time traveling forward into the future—and in fact everyone on Earth does just that, we travel forward into the future by one year each year. The time dilation effects of special relativity allow someone who travels at close to the speed of light to take a trip which takes a lot less time from her point of view than from the point of view of an observer who stays behind on Earth . . . when she returns, only months have passed for her while years have passed for those left behind. So from her point of view, she's traveled forward into the future.

Traveling back into the past is a completely different story, however. While nothing in Einstein's work explicitly rules out time travel into the past, nothing supports it, either. One of the biggest problems with time travel into the past is causality—the present is built up out of a series of past events, so what happens if someone goes back in time to change things? This conundrum has been the subject of numerous science fiction movies and novels over the years, but is actually an important topic of serious scientific research as well. Currently, the jury is out—we just aren't sure yet if time travel to the past is actually possible.

62. WHY IS THE SKY BLUE? (CRITICAL OPALESCENCE)

Einstein was a major proponent of the "thought-experiment," the idea that by letting his mind wander and explore, he could determine answers to questions that were seemingly unsolvable. Einstein realized that downtime, creative thought, and imagination were necessary to the evolution of advanced ideas. Not only that, but he reasoned that an enormously complex idea could usually be boiled down to a simple, clean core by clearing one's mind of preconceptions. He probably got into trouble for staring out the classroom window during elementary school, but it sure paid off later. One of his typical thought-experiments was in the area of solving a common riddle: Why is the sky blue?

In 1911, early in his career, Einstein thought extensively about this problem. In a paper on critical opalescence, he calculated a formula for the way that light molecules scattered, and his equations were proven true experimentally. As scientists now know, the different colors of light are distinguished by their wavelengths. The sky looks blue on a cloudless day because molecules scatter blue light in the air more than red light. When we look at the sun, it appears white because it's a mixture of all colors along the spectrum.

Einstein, of course, wasn't the first scientist to try to tackle this problem. In the seventeenth century, Isaac Newton used prisms to determine how light is split on the spectrum. Prisms, as they are well known today, are pieces of glass or quartz that are usually triangular in shape; they look like three-dimensional wedges. Prisms are used to deviate a beam of light as it passes through the prism. Light is split by color as it exits the prism. They can also be used to invert images, so that they appear upside down.

John Tyndall, an Irish physicist working in the mid-nineteenth century, discovered that blue wavelengths, which are relatively short, are scattered more strongly than red. Einstein built upon these previous scientists' research and provided one of the first concrete ways in which this age-old riddle could be solved.

Critical opalescence is a topic Einstein discussed in a paper he wrote in 1911. This concept has to do with the way light scatters near the liquid-gas critical point. Density fluctuations can be extreme, and the point at which a fluid becomes almost opaque is called "critical opalescence." Imagine, for example, pouring water into a teakettle and then sealing the kettle. Bring the water to boiling, and the water will start turning to gas. Eventually, there will be a point where the densities of the liquid and gas are about the same; the fluid will start to look like it's clouded over, and this is the point that interested Einstein.

In addition to studying and deciphering the technicalities behind a blue sky, it's possible to extrapolate into the nature of Einstein's thought-experiment. If he was trying to figure out why the sky is blue, it's reasonable to assume that he also thought of why the sky was NOT blue. Nighttime, for example, yielded a nonblue sky, as did sunrise and sunset. By taking a step back and thinking of the problem from many different angles, eventually Einstein was able to get to a point where detailed science came back into play.

Interestingly enough, it turns out that Earth's blue sky is a particularly terrestrial feature. When the first spacecraft landed on the surface of Mars in the 1970s, the first color pictures they sent back were automatically adjusted to make the sky appear blue. It turned out, however, that because of the different density and dust content of the Martian atmosphere, the sky on Mars is actually closer to pink. The pictures were quickly readjusted to show the real colors of the Martian sky. It's interesting to wonder if Einstein would have predicted a pink sky for Mars.

63. Wormholes

Do actual earthworms travel through wormholes? Probably, but "wormhole" has a specific meaning when talking about space and physics. A wormhole is a construct that can be thought of as a tunnel in space. Any type of matter can go through this tunnel, and it can go literally in any dimensions—wormholes are thought to exist in "our" three dimensions (X, Y, and Z), with the addition of time as the fourth dimension.

Take a look at a leaf, and consider this as a plane in space. Imagine a bug (say a worm) was crawling from the stem down the leaf, trying to get off the edge. The normal course of action for the bug would be to traverse the leaf, crawling all the way across it, until it fell off an edge. Now imagine the leaf curled up, so that the bug could just crawl straight down (through space), and off the edge of the leaf. Wouldn't that be much faster? Think of a wormhole in the same way: when space is curved, there's much less time (and space) between points A and B.

The idea of a wormhole is as old as general relativity itself. Soon after Einstein published his finalized version of general relativity, in 1916, an Austrian scientist named Ludwig Flamm studied Karl Schwarzschild's solutions to Einstein's equations. While Schwarzschild had theorized that black holes could exist, Flamm took the notion a step further to realize that in fact, instead of just being a single point in space, a black hole could actually have two ends, connecting two parts of the same universe or even two different universes. If material falls into the "black hole" end, it can be expelled out of

$\Sigma\theta'\frac{i}{\pi\lambda}\lambda \ ^{a}\frac{2}{7\theta}\Delta\frac{\sigma}{\pi} \ ^{\chi}\Delta\pi\theta\Delta\Sigma\theta'\frac{i}{\pi\lambda}\lambda \ ^{a}\frac{2}{7\theta}\Delta\frac{\sigma}{\pi}\chi\Delta\pi\Sigma\theta\frac{i}{\pi\lambda}\lambda \ ^{a}\frac{2}{7\theta}\Delta\frac{\sigma}{\pi}\chi\Delta\pi\theta\Delta^{\sigma}$

the other end in a so-called "white hole". The tunnel connecting two completely different parts of the universe is called a wormhole.

Einstein studied these strange properties of wormholes with Nathan Rosen at Princeton, in the 1930s. He called this concept an "Einstein-Rosen bridge". Still, these connections were mainly just mathematical curiosities until the late American professor of astronomy and author Carl Sagan was writing his novel "Contact" in the 1980s. Sagan wanted a way for his main character to travel immense distances through space without violating the laws of physics, and worked with Caltech physicist Kip Thorne. Through this work, Thorne and his graduate students realized that it would be theoretically possible for a human to travel from one part of the universe to another through a wormhole.

Of course, there are also disadvantages to this mode of travel. One is that the wormholes are inherently unstable, and prone to collapse. In addition, it's possible that travel at a speed faster than the speed of light would be required at some point in the journey, which violates the laws of physics. Some scientists, including Stephen Hawking, have investigated whether there seems to be any way to stabilize a wormhole, and have concluded that it is unlikely that any method known to today's physics could do so. It is possible that quantum mechanical effects could stabilize wormholes for brief periods of time, but it is unlikely that these tiny effects could be amplified sufficiently to allow us to travel through wormholes.

Another strange property of wormholes is that some theories have suggested they could be not only spatial but also temporal gateways, opening to another place and time in the universe. Stephen Hawking has argued against time travel being a true possibility with wormholes, however, stating that quantum mechanics would basically prevent time travel from taking place.

In any case, while black holes have recently been detected, wormholes remain purely theoretical constructs. Until we actually find and study a wormhole, we will never fully understand their properties and potential.

Part 4
War, Religion, and Politics

Einstein's name brings many images to mind. His wild hair, his great intellect, his impact on science that will likely last for centuries; all of these things are ideas that are easily associated with Albert Einstein's life and work.

Political awareness. Activisim. Patriotism. Social Responsibility. Such traits are more likely to be associated with Martin Luther King Jr., FDR, or Susan B. Anthony. Yet Einstein was all of these things and more. His participation in political events were shaped by both a sense of intellectual obligation and his own experience of having to flee Europe during the rise of the Nazi Party.

Seeing himself as a man of reason, Einstein often expressed his belief that anyone carrying the gift of intelligence should also have an obligation to use it for the improvement of the world. In the pages ahead, you'll see that he did more than was expected of him to live up to that ideal.

64. Einstein the pacifist

The seeds of Einstein's pacifism were planted during his return to the Eid-genössische Technische Hochschule (ETH)—which he'd actually strug-gled to graduate from—in 1912. There he met Friedrich Adler, a famous Austrian physicist. Adler was also a pacifist, and one who was vehemently opposed to the impending war. His antiwar ideas rubbed off on Einstein, and they continued to influence him for years to come. Adler would later become more notorious than famous. He actually assassinated the prime minister of Austria in 1916.

There was a bit of competition between the two men, as well. Adler was offered a teaching position at the University of Zurich in 1908, the same position Einstein applied for (and was first rejected for). Adler declined the offer, saying that the university was ridiculous for rejecting Einstein. Adler was also responsible for introducing Einstein to the Sec-ond International, a political group consisting of socialist and democratic Europeans. While Einstein solidified some of his growing pacifistic ideas here, the group was always divided amongst itself and never gained wide-spread popularity. Though Einstein and Adler met through science, they discovered much other common ground and respect appears to have been paramount during their relationship.

Throughout his life, Einstein spoke about pacifism and the dangers of the growing martial thinking of governments. Einstein called his brand of pacifism "militant pacifism", and tried to draw a stark distinction between the naïve view of pacifism as weak and passive, as opposed to his more active definition of pacifism as a responsibility to educate our children about the dangers of war. Especially once he moved to the United States, he spoke out eloquently against militarism and for the prevention of war rather than the preparation for war. Einstein also provided counsel for draft resisters, stating that conscientious objectors had a moral obligation to not only personally refuse to join the military, but speak out against all types of war and militarism to others.

For Einstein, his belief in nonviolence would be tested as his devotion to his ideals put him at odds with a new group coming to power in Germany after World War I: the Nazi party (see number 68).

Later in his life, Einstein would become involved with various groups specifically focused on promoting peace. One example was the Jewish Peace Fellowship, a group of Jews that promoted worldwide peace through positive action. The group was founded in 1941 to support Jews who didn't want to serve in the military. Einstein believed it was their right to be supported as Jews, and again simply as citizens who chose a certain path.

After World War II, when asked by an interviewer whether violence was just a part of the human condition and therefore inevitable, Einstein disagreed. He responded that while violence was undoubtedly part of human nature, it was our responsibility as humans to try to channel and control that impulse as much as possible and to build institutions to allow for peaceful rather than violent resolutions to conflicts.

65. Einstein and Judaism

Some background on Judaism is essential for understanding Einstein's complex relationship with the religion into which he was born. The Jewish religion is one of the world's oldest and is the foundation for many other religions. The holy work of Judaism is the Torah, referred to in Christianity as the Old Testament of the Bible. In the books of the Torah, which were handed down through the generations by an oral tradition (and eventually written down, of course) the basic principles of the religion were set forth, including the idea that God exists, there is just one God, and God is the only entity that should be prayed to. God would reward people who believed in Him and followed His word, and would punish those who did otherwise. God allowed for a prophet named Moses to communicate His will to the people. Through Moses, God issued the Ten Commandments, the rules that became the guiding moral principles for the Jewish faith. They include such ideas as not killing, not stealing, honoring your father and mother, not committing adultery, and keeping the Sabbath day holy.

One of the defining characteristics of Judaism, as compared to other religions, is its very lack of definition. While the basics of Judaism are clear, much of the rest of the religion is left undefined. There is no official Jewish doctrine on the afterlife (that is, there is no concept of Heaven or its less-friendly alternative) or, other than the Commandments, on how people should pray or otherwise live their lives.

$$\Sigma \theta_{\pi\lambda}^{'\dot{z}} \ ^{\omega\prime}_{\pi}\theta \Delta_{\Sigma}^{\sigma} \ \chi_{\Delta}^{\dot{\sigma}}\pi \ \theta_{\Delta} \Sigma \theta_{\pi\lambda}^{'\lambda} \ ^{\omega\prime}_{\pi}\theta \Delta_{\Sigma}^{\sigma}\pi \ \chi \ \Delta^{\sigma}\pi \Sigma \theta \ ^{\alpha}_{\pi\lambda} \ ^{\omega\prime}_{\pi}\theta \Delta_{\Sigma}^{\sigma}\pi \ \chi \ \Delta^{\sigma}\pi \ \theta_{\Delta} \ ^{\alpha}$$

In this respect, the Jewish faith presented an interesting conflict to Einstein. On the one hand, there are a few hard-and-fast tenets of the religion that are basically non-negotiable. On the other hand, Judaism leaves much to interpretation, and each Jew is responsible for figuring certain things out for herself. Judaism is also a cultural tradition as well as a religious one, due to the shared values and mores passed down through generations of Jews. These include foods, language, charity, and many others.

Einstein was more of a cultural Jew than a religious one. Although he was born Jewish and raised in a Jewish household, the religion did not dominate his upbringing. Quite the contrary, in fact. Einstein was raised in Ulm, Germany, a town known for its Jewish residents who assimilated enough into German society not to be persecuted. Einstein's family didn't raise him to be a closet Jew, though—they simply don't seem to have been active practitioners of the religion.

When the Einstein clan moved to Munich during Einstein's early years, in fact, they didn't fit into the Jewish community there because they were so unobservant. Einstein never had a bar mitzvah, the traditional Jewish confirmation and recitation. This ceremony is performed by Jewish male children at the culmination of their Hebrew education, usually around their thirteenth birthday. The fact that he didn't participate in this Jewish ritual indicates his desire to interpret and create his own Judaism, even at a young age.

Einstein also never practiced stereotypical Judaism in his adult life. He didn't seem to have attended regular synagogue services, and he definitely took issue with many aspects of Torah-based Judaism, including its conception and definition of God. However, Einstein was extremely connected to Jewish views on values, ethics, and morality. The emphasis on personal responsibility for religion also appealed to Einstein's fundamental nature. Had Judaism been more stringent the way some religions are, Einstein might have rejected it altogether. Throughout his life, he developed his own approach to Judaism, which is entirely in keeping with the very spirit of the religion.

66. Einstein's views on God

When looking at Einstein's belief in the Jewish notion of one God, the great physicist veered once again from the traditional. In this area he followed the teachings of Baruch Spinoza (1632–1677), a European rationalist philosopher. Spinoza was himself Jewish, although he rejected many of the principles of Orthodox Judaism. Philosophically he held that humans were driven by the desire to stay alive. Self-preservation outlawed free will almost completely. Thinking and understanding separated good (intelligent) people from evil (and, consequently, unintelligent) ones. He described God as true thought, and the only way to know God was through thought and understanding.

As part of this system of beliefs, all nature was considered God. Einstein had always had a secondary interest in nature, loving outdoor activities and simply taking in all that nature had to offer. However, "nature" meant more than trees and waterfalls. For Einstein, nature represented order, harmony, and unity. He once said that he believed in Spinoza's God, one who was concerned with the physicality of the world rather than with determining the fate of mankind.

Einstein's fascination with Spinoza while not representing a complete break with the Jewish tradition, was enough of a stretch that he would never have been considered a proponent of "true" Judaism. This idea is not entirely inconsistent with the New Age approach to religion, which holds that God is a part of every creature.

Judaism and science were, without question, two of the most important aspects of Einstein's life. Religion and science have historically been at odds with each other; Einstein, however, had a unique take on religion that would allow him to reconcile these two distinct aspects of his personal and professional life.

So, how did he do it? First off, Einstein believed that emotion was the primary motivator behind human action. Desire led people to act, in his rationale, as did fear, happiness, guilt, and other human characteristics. Love and fear were perhaps the two most powerful motivators for Einstein. Children loved and feared their parents, and these emotions stimulated their actions and the communities they formed. Similarly, religious adults (or those who believed in the existence of a God) exercised these same emotions toward their God of choice.

Einstein saw Judaism predominantly as a "religion of morals," one in which people were urged to behave ethically because it was the right thing to do. His alternative, the "religion of fear," was one in which God was a terrible figure who forced people to behave against the threat of punishment, either now or in the afterlife. The Jewish scriptures, though setting out certain guidelines about God, were quite open to interpretation. Their lack of fear-inducing dogma left interpretation of morality up to the individual, something Einstein intensely appreciated about Judaism.

Following from this idea that Judaism and ethics are compatible, Einstein also argued that science and Judaism could influence each other beneficially. Religion and science were historically incompatible, he argued, because either events happened for scientific reasons, or a God intervened to make events happen. How could both ideas exist simultaneously?

Einstein reasoned that a religious scientist like himself was one who, while incredibly awestruck at the magnitude of the Earth's creation, was completely driven by the desire to understand it. In Einstein's world, faith could belong to both nature and science, to both God and technology. Einstein himself wrote that he longed to understand God's actions as well as His thoughts. He wasn't necessarily concerned with dissecting mysticism and faith, but he wanted to know how God had created the universe. He believed and accepted the idea of a power higher than himself. Being Einstein, though, he wasn't content to leave it at that. He was always searching for comprehension, and this desire for understanding was not limited to the realm of hard science.

Judaism was not the only religion that Einstein considered in his multifaceted approach to science. He made connections between science and other religions as well. He thought Buddhism reflected science and research quite accurately. This idea is actually not surprising in light of Einstein's theory of relativity. For Einstein, waves and vibrations replaced the hard substance that other scientists liked to attribute to the world, and this notion of the world (as more conceptual than absolute) fit well with the teachings of Buddhism. In addition, Buddhism transcends the notion of an individual, all-power God, and Einstein agreed with this aspect.

One of the most typical divisions between religion and science occurs with the subject of how life began, or the debate between evolution and creationism.

What did Einstein think about this great debate? His theory of relativity worked toward defining space and time, two of the most abstract concepts there are. A true creationist would probably consider such research blasphemous, since to some extent it subverts the notion of an infinite God and an equally infinite universe. However, Einstein seems to have held with the existence of some force that was responsible for creating the universe, though probably not the traditional Judeo-Christian one. He was constantly amazed by the miracle of the world as it was shown through science and understanding.

67. How did WWI affect Einstein?

World War I officially began on June 28, 1914. A Slav citizen named Gavrilo Princip assassinated Archduke Francis Ferdinand, who was to become king of the Austro-Hungarian Empire. Ferdinand's supporters immediately blamed Serbia for the attack, and thus began the war. Britain officially entered the war on August 4, 1914, when Germany invaded Belgium (a neutral country, although one the British had sworn to protect). Trenches were dug, and machine guns were set up; the land war proceeded throughout this part of Europe.

However, the war was not limited to the mainland continent of Europe. Japan soon allied itself with the Allied Powers, and the Ottoman Empire with the Central Powers. Other countries and nations joined in, hence the name World War I. It truly became a worldwide affair, one that affected just about everyone.

During the period in 1915, the United States made loans to Britain. Since most European men of working age had been drafted or voluntarily joined the service, women were taking over traditional men's roles back home in their communities. Bulgaria joined the Central Forces, and Italy switched sides to fight with the Allied Forces. Also in 1915, German Zeppelin airships dropped bombs over Britain. Submarine warfare was also an element, making this war truly a "world war" fought on land, in the sea, and in the air. The United States declared war on Germany in 1917 and, to make a very long story short, in 1918, an armistice was signed between Germany and the Allied Forces.

So how did World War I affect Einstein? For one thing, it brought out the pacifism in him that had been somewhat latent in previous years. Einstein had always had pacifist tendencies and had successfully avoided serving in either the German or Swiss military during his youth. The breadth of the war, and the influence it had on just about every aspect of European life, made Einstein realize how little he wanted to be involved with the fighting.

The war also brought about a change in priorities for Einstein. He had, up until this point, been obsessed largely with science and research. Family provided a happy diversion, as did his day job at the patent office, but science was first and foremost upon his mind. The devastating and far-reaching impact of World War I made Einstein much more aware of the importance of politics. His political consciousness was born in this period. Politics occupied more and more of Einstein's time, particularly in the middle years of the war.

His discontent with the war did not earn him new friends in the academic community. Einstein was horrified by what he saw as the "civilized" nations of Europe engaging in down-and-dirty, primal battle. However, many of Einstein's colleagues were either of a military background or otherwise pro-war. Still a Swiss citizen, Einstein was in no danger of having to fight for Germany, but his political views were definitely solidified during this period.

At the start of the war, a coalition of German scientists and other intellectuals signed a manifesto in support of Germany's position in the war. Einstein, on the other hand, signed antiwar petitions. His pacifism probably offended some of his contemporaries and contributed to a growing personal alienation Einstein felt, both in his marriage and in his professional life.

The year 1914 when the war first broke out, heralded several important changes in Einstein's life. It was then that he was invited by Max Planck to become director of the Kaiser Wilhelm Institute of Physics, a position he accepted and would retain until 1933. This organization was an opportunity for Einstein to conduct his own science and research, under his own demands, schedules, and guidelines.

Like Einstein, Planck was a pacifist. Although projects relating to war were plentiful during his lifetime, Planck refused to work on any project whose research went directly to the war effort. He adamantly opposed Hitler and anti-Semitism in general. Although he was reluctant to return to Germany at all, Einstein was wooed there by the promise of a prestigious position at the center of the European physics community. In addition to the position at Kaiser Wilhelm, Einstein was also appointed a professor at the University of Berlin in 1914, furthering both his academic and research goals.

68. Einstein and the Nazi party

Following 1919 and the end of World War I, the Nazi party gained tremendous strength in Germany. Anti-Semitism would come to its peak during this period. Einstein was a target because he was Jewish, and his theory of relativity was dubbed "Jewish Communist." He was increasingly hounded by the Nazis, and their actions led him to become a more outspoken public Jew. He worked with anti-Fascist groups in Germany, making himself more and more of a target. Not having been raised in an observant household, he was hesitant to join Jewish organizations, but he was firmly convinced that the Nazi beliefs and tactics were hateful and wrong.

The impact of the Nazi regime on German Jews grew more and more pervasive, and ultimately Einstein was forced to flee the country. Friends and family feared for his safety, and the move was probably none too soon. His leaving was, in addition to a security measure, a sign of protest—Adolf Hitler was appointed chancellor of Germany in 1933.

His emigration in 1933 wasn't the first time Einstein had been in the United States. He actually visited in 1921 and delivered lectures on relativity at Princeton University as part of the Stafford Little series. He was also given an honorary degree at this time. The main reason Einstein went to America at that point was to promote Zionism, but his scientific lectures proved immensely popular. They were published in a book by Princeton University Press in 1921, *The Meaning of Relativity*. Between 1930 and 1933, Einstein alternated between the United States and Europe. He spent summers in Caputh (a town near Berlin), winters teaching at the California Institute of Technology (located in southern California), and each spring in Berlin.

Einstein was in his mid-fifties when he and his family moved to America, arriving there on October 17, 1933. In doing so, he gave up his German citizenship, at which point the German government took all the property he still had there. As the Nazis continued their rise to power, and the atrocities they committed began to be recognized by the rest of the world, Einstein's view of the situation changed, and his stance hardened.

Eventually, Einstein was so vehemently opposed to the Nazi regime that he issued a statement after his permanent move to the United States that the rest of Europe should defend itself against Hitler. For the first time, he entertained the possibility that the use of force might be acceptable, and, in fact, completely necessary. This change in his viewpoint did not endear him to more diehard pacifists, once again placing Einstein in between worlds, and aligned clearly with neither side. Some pacifists were shocked at Einstein's apparent reversal. He defended himself, however, by saying essentially that while he still hated violence and armies, that hatred was overridden by his fear of what a successful Nazi regime could do to the world. In retrospect it's easy to see that there was really no other decision to make at the time—Nazi Germany had to be stopped, at just about any cost. Still, while there were those who were disappointed in Einstein's apparent wavering, the situation can instead be seen as further evidence of the adaptability of Einstein's beliefs and his overall pragmatism.

69. Einstein's work with refugees

Being such a famous and important figure, it was easier for Einstein to get his family out from under the growing oppression of the Nazi regime in Europe. He was able, along with other prominent scientists and intellectuals, to escape with his life—something many European Jews were not able to do. Those Jews who were able to escape found themselves penniless, for they were not permitted to bring any personal assets other than a suitcase of clothing and other small items—cash, bonds, and other money were not allowed to leave the country. And not only did they escape into poverty, but many had no place to escape to since most other countries, especially those outside of Europe, were not accepting Jewish immigrants. While Einstein made it to America and continued his life relatively unscathed, he was keenly aware of how fortunate he was compared to many of the Jews left behind.

Shortly after his move to the United States in 1933, Einstein helped found the International Rescue Committee (IRC). The IRC is a nonprofit group still in existence. It exists to help refugees from around the world and especially aids people who are trying to escape racial and religious persecution. The group itself is voluntary and nonprofit so, in accordance with Einstein's wishes, it really exists solely to help people.

When there is a national emergency somewhere in the world and people have to flee their homeland, the IRC springs into action. They provide a number of important services such as food, medical care, emergency shelter, and other forms of sanctuary. They also help refugees get settled into their new lives, offering training and educational programs. While they will assist with a refugee's attempt to return to their native land, they continue assistance in a new country if a return to the old one isn't possible. As one who fled and abandoned his former home, Einstein would probably have been very pleased with the way this organization developed and blossomed.

There were several offshoots of the IRC. The American branch of the IRC (known in Europe as the International Relief Association) was created specifically for helping Jews fleeing from Hitler's Germany. There was also a branch called the Emergency Rescue Committee (ERC) that was developed mostly for helping European refugees in Vichy, France. The American and European branches (IRC and ERC) came together

$$\Sigma \theta_{\pi\Lambda}^{\prime\lambda} {}^{\sigma}\!\!\stackrel{\lambda}{\theta} \qquad {}^{\alpha}\!\pi\,\theta_\Delta\Sigma\theta_{\pi\Lambda}^{\prime\lambda} {}^{\sigma}\!\!\stackrel{\lambda}{\theta}\!\stackrel{\sigma}{\Delta}\!\stackrel{\chi}{\pi}\!\stackrel{\Delta}{\Delta}\!\pi\Sigma\theta \stackrel{u}{\pi\Lambda}^{\lambda} {}^{\sigma}\!\!\stackrel{\lambda}{\theta}\!\stackrel{\sigma}{\Delta}\!\stackrel{\chi}{\pi}\!\stackrel{\Delta}{\Delta}\!\pi\,\theta_\Delta^{\;\alpha}$$

under one organization in 1942. Throughout the years, Einstein's group has helped many people from many different countries, including South Vietnam, Hungary, Cuba, Chile, and Yugoslavia. They have also set up healthcare programs in countries such as Poland and El Salvador.

70. WHY EINSTEIN WROTE A LETTER TO PRESIDENT ROOSEVELT

The year 1939 was a seminal one in world history. The discovery of the fission of uranium had caused newspapers and magazines in the United States to start to discuss atomic energy as a popular topic, but the subject had yet to be verified and examined by physicists. In fact, few scientists took the prospect of atomic energy seriously at this point. However, Einstein and other scientists (including Leo Szilard, Edward Teller, and Eugene Wigner) recognized the need for America to unite in its pursuit of such research, and eventually they decided to collaborate on a letter addressed to President Franklin D. Roosevelt. Understanding that they needed support and name recognition for their effort to succeed, Szilard, Teller, and Wigner came to Einstein with the idea of writing to the president.

The circumstances of this initial meeting were less official than one might think for such a serious subject. Einstein was supposedly sailing at the time and greeted his friends at the dock dressed in his typical sailing garb. He invited his colleagues to sit on his porch, where Szilard presented the problem that lay before them: if America did not begin the quest to uncover the secrets of atomic energy, someone else, and someone more dangerous, would do so first. While he was a devoted pacifist who was fundamentally opposed to creating weapons, Einstein understood the obvious problem that would arise if the Nazis developed this technology first, and he agreed to join forces with the other scientists in taking action.

In the letter that they crafted to President Roosevelt, the scientists informed the president about the state of scientific research into nuclear fission. They suggested that it might be possible to incorporate this new science into weapons of unprecedented power. They recommended experimentation on a large scale before even attempting to create such a device. Einstein probably dictated this letter in German, which was then translated by Szilard before sending it on to the president. The letter was dated August 2, 1939, but was probably not actually presented to the president until October 11—more than a month after World War II began with Germany's invasion of Poland. It appears unclear whether the letter, however well-intentioned, actually had much effect.

President Roosevelt eventually would create funding and opportunity for the research that could create nuclear weapons. The Briggs Committee was formed in 1939 for the purpose of studying chain reactions with uranium, an essential component of a nuclear weapon. Research went slowly because, at the time, it was still considered fairly abstract research—not something that anyone intended to use in a war. The pace was picked up after a British report in 1941, one that showed that an atomic bomb could in fact be built and ready for use in just a few years.

71. WAS EINSTEIN RESPONSIBLE FOR THE ATOMIC BOMB?

To put it in the clearest possible words, Einstein opposed using the atomic bomb. He was still fundamentally opposed to war, and he was not in favor of using a nuclear weapon to bomb another country. He stated several times that he thought the United States should demonstrate the atomic bomb to foreign countries, not use it to destroy them. Despite the unfortunate way that history sometimes remembers Einstein's contribution here, he was quite clear in his intent.

Everyone knows that sometimes, people get blamed for things that were not their fault. Einstein is another unfortunate victim of this incorrect attribution of responsibility. Despite the truth of Einstein's involvement (or lack thereof) with the creation of the bomb, many people thought that he was entirely responsible for its design. Some even thought that $E = mc^2$ represented a formula for building a bomb. What that formula represents is how much energy can be liberated from matter; this fundamental relationship is required to determine the energy released in the explosion of an atomic bomb. However, the significance of the equation ends there, and this formula certainly does not represent a map for constructing such a bomb.

How did such a misunderstanding become prevalent? Possibly because Einstein was so famous at the time, people who didn't understand the science of nuclear fission simply thought that Einstein must be responsible for it. Perhaps there was some latent anti-Semitism at play as well. However, time and fact would prove these rumors false, and the true nature of Einstein's involvement with the project, or lack thereof, would eventually become known.

The effort to gather research and design toward the creation of the atomic bomb was managed by Vannevar Bush, an engineer and inventor who was chairman of the National Advisory Committee for Aeronautics in the late 1930s under President Roosevelt. He also proposed, and was named chairman of, the National Defense Resource Committee (NDRC), and he would eventually become military science and research advisor to the president. In his work for the NDRC, Vannevar Bush was responsible for consolidating military science operations and bringing them under the auspices of this organization. The most notable research to be contained under this new group was that of the Uranium Committee, which first studied the potential of the atomic bomb.

Bush's role in the development of the atomic bomb cannot be underestimated. It was he who convinced the president that other countries could create such a bomb, and that the United States must develop one first. December 1941 marked the year that manufacturing plants, ones where fissionable material could be created, were starting to be built. In June 1942, responsibility for the development of the atomic bomb was given to the U.S. Army. It is clear, then, that both Bush and the U.S. government held far more responsibility for the making of the bomb than Einstein ever could have held.

72. Einstein rejected for the Manhattan Project

When it came time to actually construct a location capable of containing the birthplace of the atomic bomb, the U.S. government looked long and hard for a suitable place to build such a facility. It couldn't be located near any international borders, and it also couldn't be too near major residential areas. Everyone understood what could happen if there was an accident, and officials wanted to minimize any potential risks to American citizens. Los Alamos, New Mexico, was eventually decided upon as the best location, and a scientist named J. Robert Oppenheimer was chosen to lead the endeavor that would come to be called the Manhattan Project.

Twenty-seven months later, the United States had achieved what had previously been considered impossible. This endeavor took place on an enormous scale—the factory in Los Alamos soon outgrew that of the General Motors plant. Quite impressive for something that was supposed to have been a secret.

While Einstein was consulted at various points and times about the development of an atomic weapon, he was not chosen to be part of the project, making him one of many experts who were rejected. One of the main reasons for such a decision was the tremendous need to protect the security of the project. America was at war, and everything was done in complete secrecy, and even the families of the scientists working on it had to be kept in the dark. There were over 600 scientists working on the creation of the atomic bomb—that's a lot of people to try to keep quiet. Their mail was screened, their cars had special license plates so they could easily be identified, and family photos couldn't show anything about their location. The government took all these precautions because they were worried that Germany or another foreign enemy would discover their location. While the exact reasons for Einstein's disengagement from the project may never be known, it is suspected that his obviously pacifist leanings were a major factor in his elimination from the team.

Einstein also wasn't the only Jewish person involved in some way with the Manhattan Project. Several of the other scientists were German Jews as well, including Edward Teller (who helped write the letter to President Roosevelt that started the entire campaign). Felix Bloch and Otto Frisch were instrumental in the creation of the bomb, as was Enrico Fermi (an Italian scientist who would go on to become extremely famous for his work on quantum mechanics and atomic structure). Fermi actually won the 1938 Nobel Prize in physics for his work in this area.

As Einstein was painfully aware, the Manhattan Project represented a mixed blessing of major proportions. On the negative side, of course, were the deadly effects on Hiroshima and Nagasaki. These consequences cannot be mitigated by the research that went into the project, of course, but it is important to realize that the Manhattan Project allowed scientists to discover secrets of atomic energy that had been previously unexplained, leading to peaceful uses to provide electricity, for instance.

73. Einstein's Reaction to Hiroshima and Nagasaki

The atomic bomb was first tested in the middle of 1945. President Roosevelt died in April 1945, though, and was succeeded by President Harry Truman. Political leaders in America became convinced that they had to attack or invade Japan in order to win the war, and Truman decided to use the atomic bomb. General Dwight Eisenhower, who would later become president, was commanding the Allied Forces in Europe at this time. President Truman gave the order to drop the atomic bomb over Hiroshima in August 1945, despite the fact that large-scale testing had not been conducted. No one was sure exactly what would happen. The impact, of course, was monumental. An incredibly bright explosion ensued, and some estimate that as many as 80,000 people were killed instantly, while many more were killed over the months and years following the explosion by the effects of the radiation. Winds and fires followed, destroying much of the Japanese-style wooden architecture in the area. Nagasaki was bombed as well, and Japan surrendered the following week.

Einstein's first public reaction to the bombing of Hiroshima and Nagasaki came nearly a year after the events. In a 1946 article published in the *New York Times,* Einstein said that he didn't think President Roosevelt would have authorized the bombings if he had still been alive.

Einstein would later declare that the one great mistake of his life was signing the letter to then-President Roosevelt, suggesting that atomic bombs could be made (see number 70). Had he known about the devastation that would ensue, he said that he would have rather spent his life as a shoemaker. His ongoing justification for having signed that letter was that, to the end, it was better than what would have happened if Germany had developed the atomic bomb first. Einstein witnessed the Nazi oppression first hand, and he was convinced that their usage of the atomic bomb would have been far more disastrous than anything that might happen at the hands of the Americans.

It is unclear whether he still agreed with this position after the bombings of Hiroshima and Nagasaki, though. Supposedly, when Einstein first heard of the bombings, he cried out loud—probably as much for the fear of what could happen, as what had already happened. He went so far as to say that "avoiding a world catastrophe" was one of the most important things to be aware of in the exploration of the atomic bomb.

One of the most far-reaching legacies of American atomic bomb development was the ensuing arms race. Now that the United States had this capability, other countries wanted the same weapons to be able to compete on the same level, should it ever become necessary. While one of the United States' primary nuclear rivals became the Soviet Union (USSR), other countries also hurried to develop their own nuclear weapons, thereby increasing tension felt throughout the world and leading up to what would become the Cold War.

74. EINSTEIN'S ANTINUCLEAR WORK CONTINUED BY BERTRAND RUSSELL

By 1943 the Soviets, having learned of the Manhattan Project, set about researching and developing their own atomic bomb. After World War II ended, the United States implemented a policy of disarmament, where all materials that could be used for nuclear fission would be given to an international agency. The Soviet Union, in contrast, wanted to completely destroy all nuclear weapons already in existence, a policy the United States didn't agree with.

Additional tensions between the Soviet Union and America were fueled by this disagreement. The USSR was a Communist country, while the United States was a democracy; most people at the time agreed that these two types of government were completely incompatible with each other. The United States declared a sort of general war against Communism by providing funding for non-Communist countries, and the Cold War was informally declared by the stating of these ideas in the Truman Doctrine of 1947.

The North Atlantic Treaty Organization (NATO) was created in 1949. Its initial member countries were the United States, France, Britain, the Netherlands, Belgium, and Luxembourg. One of the main goals of NATO was to unite against Stalin, whom many thought could become the next Hitler. In 1950, the United States passed a resolution called NSC-68, the gist of which was to increase national defense spending dramatically and to not allow the Soviets to dominate the world the way Germany had tried to. All these factors contributed to the Cold War, which would last until the early 1990s, when the Soviet Union dissolved.

American experimentation into new kinds of warfare certainly didn't end with World War II. In 1952, Americans tested the first hydrogen bomb at Enewetak Atoll in the Marshall Islands. The Soviets followed with a thermonuclear weapon, and the British succeeded with their own in 1957. The United States followed the Soviet launch with the creation and deployment of the world's first nuclear-powered ship. Other experiments by other countries would follow.

Einstein feared that the growing Cold War would threaten democracy, even within the United States. His fears were realized by the creation of the House Un-American Activities Committee (HUAC) in 1938, which lasted until 1975. This committee was part of the House of Representatives, and its goal was to investigate anyone and anything considered disloyal to the United States, nominally in the name of anti-Communism. People were questioned and trials were held. Einstein was generally correct that this sort of extended fear of Communism really threatened the freedom that had once characterized America.

Meanwhile, public opposition to the increasing nuclear arms race was growing. In the spring of 1955, shortly before his death, Einstein collaborated with Bertrand Russell (1872–1970). Russell was a British philosopher and mathematician who publicly condemned the hydrogen bomb tests of 1954; he would work with Einstein a year later.

This campaign was Einstein's last attempt to try to convince the world that nuclear weapons posed a threat. The two issued the Russell-Einstein manifesto, in which they urged governments from all nations to stop considering the use of nuclear weapons in war. This document set up two choices: ending the human race, versus an agreement to end all wars. The latter option was combined with a caveat that no new wars be started. They suggested nuclear disarmament and wrote that, as scientists and humanitarians, they strongly favored peace.

Russell would go on to continue this work after Einstein's death in 1955. In 1958 he became the founder and president of the Campaign for Nuclear Disarmament. He would also participate in antinuclear protests, getting himself jailed more than once in the process.

While Einstein had little to do with the actual creation of the atomic bomb, he was part of the initial effort. And, of course, his scientific discovery from decades earlier laid the groundwork that other scientists would use to develop the bomb itself. It's hard to say how much responsibility Einstein ultimately felt for the devastation in Hiroshima and Nagasaki. Scientists cannot possibly predict every way in which their results will be used, nor are they necessarily responsible for what others choose to do with their results. For Einstein to have "taken it all back" he would have had to undo the discovery of $E = mc^2$, and that alone would have changed the entire course of history.

75. Einstein: president of Israel?

Given all the work he'd done for Jewish refugees during the second World War and how deeply held his belief in Judaism was, it isn't a surprise that Einstein did his best to support the betterment of Jewish people around the world. What may be surprising to some people is that one of the world's best-known scientists almost became a world leader. For someone who disliked public speaking early in his career, it certainly would have been a major lifestyle change to suddenly become head of an entire country.

Of course, such an offer didn't just appear out of the blue. Albert Einstein had been making a name for himself in many different arenas, including math and science; however, he was also a known pacifist and had already established the International Rescue Committee (IRC), to aid refugees who were forced to flee their homeland. In other words, he was acquiring a reputation as an intelligent, caring humanitarian—something that world leaders certainly should be.

In 1952, four years after the nation of Israel was founded, Einstein was officially offered the presidency of Israel. He did, however, respectfully decline this honor. As the story goes, Israel's first prime minister, David Ben-Gurion, asked Einstein to become the country's second president (a largely symbolic role) when its first president, Chaim Weizmann, died. Einstein and Dr. Weizmann had been friends, working together on fund-raising efforts for Israel. In fact, Einstein's first trip to the United States, in

1921, was with Dr. Weizmann. However, Einstein regretfully declined the invitation from Ben-Gurion.

Why did Einstein turn down this prestigious position, which really would have been the opportunity of a lifetime? Was his age the only reason Einstein didn't become president of Israel? Probably not. The real reason was more likely political. Throughout his career, Einstein had hoped that Jews and Palestinians would be able to share the land they both inhabited. His views in this area were widely misunderstood. While he may not have been explicitly opposed to the idea of creating a Jewish state, if it were to be done through warfare he probably would not have supported it.

Einstein was morally opposed to the idea of a Jewish army that would defend specifically Jewish territories because he feared the impact that such nationalism would have on the faith itself. Religion, he reasoned, should not be bound by geography and the desire to possess it. He may have picked up these inclinations from his experiences in Nazi Germany, and it's likely that he wanted to avoid becoming involved in another land war and another quest for superiority. Becoming president of Israel, even as a figurehead, might have pushed his involvement into acquisition through force, something Einstein probably wanted no part of. Still though, it must have been a very hard decision, since it is possible he could have been able to enact his ideas of pacifism if he had accepted the title of president.

76. EINSTEIN'S TIES TO ISRAEL AND JUDAISM

Despite not taking on a direct political position in the fledgling nation of Israel, Einstein did have strong connections to the land and its people. Even before being offered the presidency of Israel, Einstein was on the board of governors that planned what would come to be Hebrew University in Jerusalem. In 1922, for example, Einstein sailed to Singapore as part of a larger trip, and he used the opportunity to raise funds for Hebrew University, which had become one of his pet projects. Much of Singapore's Jewish community was reputed to have met Einstein's boat when it docked. He was very famous by this point, and he used that fame to attract both attention and funding to Jewish causes he supported. In the late 1930s, Einstein spent much time raising funds for the United Jewish Appeal, a general advocacy and awareness group for Jewish people.

In some ways, Einstein identified with Judaism more culturally than religiously. For example, the idea of extended family is very strong in the Jewish culture. All Jews are considered family. Homes are extended to those in need, and Jews tend to bond closely with other Jews. It's a cultural phenomenon that seems somewhat out of place in a fast-paced modern world, but it is nonetheless true. Einstein extended himself to offer protection and hope for maligned Jews throughout the world, as seen in his 1933 founding of the International Rescue Committee (IRC). He personally vouched for Jews coming in from Germany and other countries and offered both physical and financial support to those in need.

His support of Israel throughout World War II, as well as his active protest of the Nazi regime and the founding of the IRC, solidified his Jewish ties to Israel. He was active professionally there as well. Einstein was president of the Technion Society, Israel's first official institute of science and technology. Einstein supported the project from the very beginning, and the Technion would go on to become Israel's first university, also called the Israel Institute of Technology.

In 1925, Einstein also became the first president of the World Union of Jewish Students. This organization was founded by a Jewish man from Austria, Zvi Lauterpacht. It came about because, in some European countries, there were quotas for how many Jewish people could attend university. The match up with Einstein was obvious. Einstein was concerned about Jewish education, as well as about fighting anti-Semitism in all its forms. To a man like Albert Einstein, education and knowledge were two of the most important keys to living a full life. Learning happens throughout one's entire life, something Einstein was keenly aware of, but education is the key to opening the doors of knowledge. Einstein studied and taught for much of his life and later dedicated years to ensuring that other Jews were given those same opportunities. Einstein was involved in these and similar projects during their inception, and he truly had a huge range of influence across a variety of Jewish causes and organizations.

Part 5

Awards, Achievements, and Other Intellectual Pursuits

Einstein's achievements may have seemed radical at first, but as the global scientific community began to analyze and study his work, his reputation began to skyrocket. As this reputation grew, so too did the number of awards and honors that were bestowed upon him.

You might even consider Einstein the first "rockstar" of modern science. He traveled the world, both lecturing at universities and speaking out publicly on issues that he was passionate about. Albert was so highly regarded that one prestigious university built a department around him in an effort to entice him to stay there and continue his work.

Continue he most certainly did. Einstein's later years weren't just about lecturing. He continued his studies, diversifying his interests. The master of relativity was soon working on the forerunner for the modern hearing aid as well as a new refrigerator pump. Success certainly didn't slow him down.

77. EINSTEIN AND THE ETH

At one point, Einstein thought that he might be interested in a career in electrical engineering, like his father and brother. Despite his not having finished the German equivalent of high school, he decided to take the entrance exams to the prestigious Eidgenössische Technische Hochschule (ETH; also known as the Swiss Federal Polytechnic Institute) in 1895 in Zurich, Switzerland. This was the most famous school of its kind and, to Einstein, it represented the best in academia. However, he wasn't accepted due to poor performance on some parts of the admission exam. While he did fine on the technical and science section, he actually failed the arts and French sections. Though his French entrance essay was supposedly quite good, it was apparently not up to the standards of the Swiss instructors.

The ETH earned its reputation quickly. It was founded by the Swiss government in 1854 as a polytechnical school, accepting its first class of incoming students in 1855. The school was (and still is) divided between teaching and research; faculty members do both, and students had access to research facilities on campus. The ETH was definitely a one-of-a-kind institution. It actually remained the only national university in Switzerland until the 1960s. Today, the university is expanded and consists of two campuses—one in Zurich and one in Lausanne.

After failing to get in to the ETH, Einstein decided to attend an intermediary secondary school in Aarau, Switzerland, instead. He worked on the areas in which he'd done poorly and was determined to gain admission to the ETH. He earned a diploma in Aarau after a year, and decided to try to gain admission to the prestigious school once again.

Einstein reapplied to the ETH and was admitted in 1896. At that time, he studied to be a physics and math teacher. He graduated in 1900 at the age of twenty-one with degrees in both his primary areas of interest. Einstein loved physics and mathematics, but he was starting to realize that he would never be an outstanding overall student because he liked spending so much time in the lab. He preferred hands-on research to studying in the library, a trait that would define him throughout his life.

Einstein's years at the ETH were critical to his academic development. He was finally challenged at a high enough level that he pushed his own thinking beyond what he'd thought possible. Resources were plentiful, and, probably for the first time, he could engage in intellectual discussion with other scientists at or above his own level. It was here that Einstein first began to study the effects of bodies in motion. Although he was years away from achieving the level of discovery and understanding that would make him one of the most important scientists in history, Einstein's years at the ETH gave him the tools to begin down the path. In fact, three of his most important early scientific contributions were published just five years after his graduation, in 1905. Not too shabby for the guy who graduated with the lowest grade point average in the ETH class of 1900.

78. Einstein and the Nobel Prize

Given everything you've learned about Albert Einstein so far, what do you think he won the Nobel Prize for? When asked, most people would say that he won this prestigious award for his work on special and general relativity. And they would be completely wrong.

Today, Einstein is much better known for special and general relativity and their importance to the scientific world, but in 1921 these theories were far too controversial for the Nobel committee to consider. Instead, Einstein's solution to the problem of the photoelectric effect, and the establishment of the quantized nature of light, won him the Nobel Prize in physics.

It is interesting to note that he won the prize for his first major scientific result, and that it was for the relatively more mundane (though nonetheless revolutionary) photoelectric effect rather than for his work on relativity. The initial paper published by Einstein on the photoelectric effect was one of his early seminal works from 1905, one of his first batches of published papers ever.

Anti-Semitism may also have played a role in Einstein not receiving the Nobel Prize for relativity. In 1920, as the Nazi party gained power and influence in Germany, demonstrations interrupted many of Einstein's lectures in Berlin. Though officially denied, the protests were most likely anti-Jewish in origin. Because of the increasingly anti-Semitic overtones of German society at that time, Einstein had to defend his theories to a much greater extent than if he had been a German Nazi.

The citation for Einstein's 1921 Nobel Prize read: "For his services to Theoretical Physics, and especially for his discovery of the law of the photoelectric effect." Clearly, Einstein's breakthrough discovery, which paved the way for the development of quantum physics, was recognized by scientists worldwide.

As is befitting the enigmatic man, there was quite a bit of confusion surrounding Einstein's acceptance of the Nobel Prize. The official telegram notifying Einstein that he had won the 1921 Nobel Prize actually arrived at his home in Berlin in 1922 while he and Elsa were on their way to Japan as part of a world lecture tour. Einstein was thus unable to travel to Sweden to accept the award, which was accepted in his name by the German ambassador to Sweden. Adding to the confusion, however, was the fact that Einstein had renounced his German citizenship years ago, in 1896. Eventually, Einstein finally received his Nobel medal from the Swedish ambassador, who delivered it to Einstein in Berlin in 1923. Also in 1923, Einstein delivered his official Nobel Prize lecture in Sweden. However, rather than lecturing on the photoelectric effect, Einstein chose to speak on relativity. Interestingly enough, Einstein gave the prize money that came with the award to his ex-wife Mileva, as had been negotiated in their divorce agreement.

The impact of winning the Nobel Prize resulted in a big boost of Einstein's popularity. When Einstein and his wife Elsa toured the United States following the award, Einstein found that he had suddenly become world-famous for having won the Nobel Prize. The couple was constantly followed by photographers and journalists. Although Einstein's nature was not to pose for the camera, he used his popularity to further the two causes he felt strongest about, Zionism and pacifism.

79. How much did Einstein's first wife Mileva contribute to his Nobel Prize-winning theories?

When Einstein married his colleague Mileva Maric, it was truly a marriage of equals—at least at first. Mileva, who had been Einstein's fellow student at the Eidgenössische Technische Hochschule (ETH), was an intelligent scientist and one of just a handful of women at the institution at that time. The extent of Mileva's scientific collaborations with Einstein, however, is unknown.

Early in their married life together, during his famous time at the Swiss patent office, Einstein and Mileva appear to have at least discussed the ideas that Einstein was pondering during his off-work hours. Mileva was still trying (unsuccessfully) to finish up her degree at the ETH, as well as take care of their son Hans (born in 1904). During the years between Einstein's graduation from the ETH in 1900, and the publication of his first three major papers in 1905, what was the extent of their scientific collaboration?

Little evidence exists today that can shed light on this matter. Almost none of Mileva's letters to Einstein during this period survive in his papers, although some letters from Einstein to Mileva do endure. In some of these papers, Einstein refers to "our work" when talking to Mileva about what were perhaps their latest theories. He even mentions giving "our paper" to an eminent scientist for review. Letters that Mileva exchanged with friends during this period also have clues that perhaps she was involved in Einstein's research.

It is even possible that at least one of Einstein's famous 1905 papers was actually submitted in both Mileva's and Einstein's names. Proof resides in the word of a respected scientist, Abram Joffe, who was actually an assistant to one of the editors of the *Annals of Physics* (the journal in which Einstein's papers were published) around 1905. He stated that he saw two names on one of the papers—Marity and Einstein. Marity was another version of Maric, Mileva's maiden name.

Perhaps the greatest piece of evidence against Mileva's supposed collaboration with Einstein is simply the lack of evidence. Mileva never publicly asked for or claimed any credit for Einstein's 1905 works and never referred to herself as Einstein's collaborator on these papers. Still, she did receive the monetary award from Einstein's Nobel Prize, many years later, as one of the specifications of their divorce. Since the Nobel Prize was actually awarded for work dating back to one of those seminal 1905 papers, perhaps this was a tacit recognition of Mileva's contributions.

In 1990, a panel convened by the American Association for the Advancement of Science (AAAS), a highly respected scientific body, took up the debate. The panel considered whether there was any compelling evidence that Mileva collaborated with Einstein on the 1905 papers, but it was unable to reach a consensus on the issue. The editors of Einstein's collected papers took a similarly neutral stance—they state that while there is no explicit evidence that Mileva had a hand in this work, there is also no proof that she did not.

We will probably never know the full extent of Mileva's collaborations with Einstein. If nothing else, we know that Einstein praised her intellect and probably used her as a sounding board to bounce ideas off and help refine his theories. But it is unclear whether any of the startling innovations that made Einstein so famous actually came from the mind of his first wife.

80. EINSTEIN AND THE FOUNDING OF THE PRINCETON INSTITUTE FOR ADVANCED STUDY

The researchers and staff at Princeton University certainly knew what they wanted when it came to Albert Einstein. Einstein's relationship with the Ivy League school began when he visited in 1921 and delivered lectures on relativity as part of the Stafford Little series. Having the recently named Nobel Prize winner on hand was an opportunity that the university didn't squander.

The main reason for Einstein's trip to America at this point was to promote Zionism, but his scientific lectures proved immensely popular. They were even published in a book by Princeton University Press in 1921, *The Meaning of Relativity.* He was also given an honorary degree in physics by the university at this time. So when Einstein and his second wife Elsa moved permanently to the United States in October 1933, Princeton didn't waste any time in bringing him back to the university's New Jersey campus. Einstein was immediately offered a position there with the school's Institute for Advanced Study. The Institute had originally been founded in 1930 simply for the study of mathematics.

$\Sigma\theta^{\prime}\dot{\pi}\lambda$ $^{\alpha}\mathring{\theta}\mathring{\Delta}\frac{\sigma}{\pi}$ $^{\chi}\mathring{\Delta}^{\pi}\theta_{\Delta}$ $\Sigma\theta^{\prime}\dot{\pi}\lambda$ $^{\alpha}\mathring{\theta}\mathring{\Delta}\frac{\sigma}{\pi}^{\chi}\mathring{\Delta}^{\pi}\Sigma\theta^{\prime\prime}\dot{\pi}\lambda$ $^{\alpha}\mathring{\theta}\mathring{\Delta}\frac{\sigma}{\pi}^{\chi}\mathring{\Delta}^{\pi}\theta_{\Delta}^{\prime\prime}$

However, as soon as Einstein took on a position at Princeton, the university began to build the Institute around him, bringing in professors from various departments across the university. Formally founded in 1930 by Louis Bamberger and Caroline Bamberger Fuld, the Institute is a separate entity from Princeton. It does, of course, have many connections to the university itself. As the years progressed, the Institute widened its field to study areas such as economics and politics.

Albert Einstein had an office at the Institute, of course, which has been in constant use since his death. Most of his personal papers were left to the Hebrew University in Jerusalem, so most of them do not currently reside at the Institute. His name and spirit live on, though, including on the name of the street upon which the Institute for Advanced Study was built.

Today, the Institute for Advanced Study is a prominent part of Princeton University. Its main mission is to support learning and basic research over a range of different academic subjects. The Institute actually consists of several different schools now: the School of Historical Studies, the School of Natural Sciences, the School of Social Science, the School of Mathematics, and the Center for Systems Biology. Unlike many major study centers, the Institute does not teach from a formalized curriculum. Rather, in the spirit of Albert Einstein, it is devoted to pure research in fundamental areas of math and science. Of particular interest is their affiliation with the PBS television series, "Big Ideas," which focuses on the American interest in astronomy and physics. The Web site for the Institute is *www.ias.edu.*

81. Einstein as a University Lecturer

While it is easy to recognize Einstein's achievements as a researcher and theorist, his devotion to academics cannot be overlooked, especially when success with one helped fuel the other. After graduating from the Eidgenössische Technische Hochschule (ETH) in 1900, he, along with several classmates like Marcel Grossmann, applied for positions as teachers there only to be turned down. Einstein did manage to get a job teaching math and physics at the Technical High School in Winterthur, and there served as an Aushilfslehrer (assistant lecturer). As the next several years passed, Einstein divided his time between his low-level teaching job, his work in the patent office, and his own research. Yet in the eyes of many, including Einstein, this wasn't a very prominent teaching position.

In 1908, all that changed when Einstein was appointed Privatdozent, or lecturer, at the University of Bern. Why was he able to get a teaching job now, when he wasn't able to before? Part of the reason is that he submitted his "habilitation" thesis in this year.

In order to become a lecturer at a Swiss university, scientists were required to submit this extra thesis, which was to be completed after their doctoral theses. Einstein's habilitation was entitled "Consequences for the Constitution of Radiation Following from the Energy Distribution Law of Black Bodies." When he submitted this work, the administration at the University of Bern took notice, and Einstein was finally able to teach at a university.

As the idea of relativity began to gain recognition around this time, the outpouring of support for Einstein was comparatively enormous. The idea of making a living as a scientist was becoming more and more real. He was starting to become recognized as one of Europe's foremost scientific thinkers and researchers. It was only now that Einstein finally was able to devote his professional life more fully to science and research. In 1909, Einstein earned an associate professorship at the University of Zurich, and he was able to make a clean break with the patent office. He also resigned from his lectureship at the University of Bern.

The year 1911 brought another change for Einstein as his work led him to Prague, Czechoslovakia, where he moved beyond the associate level to become a full-fledged professor of theoretical physics at the Karl Ferdinand University. He didn't manage to spend much time in Prague, however. The very next year found Einstein back at his alma mater, the ETH, teaching and researching. In 1914, Einstein moved once again. This time it was to Berlin, Germany, where he was not only given a professorship but was also appointed the director of the Kaiser Wilhelm Institute of Physics, a position he would hold until he moved to America in 1933.

As his fame and recognition grew beyond normal academic circles, Einstein began to have an effect on educational institutions that he wasn't directly affiliated with. For example, Yeshiva University was founded in 1886, and it is the oldest Jewish university in America. In determining a name for the new college of medicine, university president Dr. Samuel Belkin was highly influenced by important scientists and politicians of the time. He ultimately chose to name the school after Einstein (called, appropriately, the Albert Einstein College of Medicine). Einstein agreed to let the school use his name in 1953, and it opened in 1955.

82. EINSTEIN'S PROFESSIONAL AFFILIATIONS

Beyond academia, Einstein's fame and genius afforded him an unusual benefit: that of public clout. Because he was a renowned expert with a solid reputation, Albert Einstein brought an extraordinary level of credibility and attention to any issue he focused on; similarly, his endorsement automatically raised the status of just about every group of which he was a member. Fortunately for the future of science, Einstein had many extracurricular activities outside of his "regular job."

For starters, Einstein had a role in one of the world's foremost science groups. The National Academy of Sciences (NAS) is an organization devoted to scientific and technological research. Chartered by Congress in 1863, part of its responsibility is to advise the government on how technology and science apply to the general public welfare. Only American citizens are permitted to be full members; all other members are considered foreign associates. Einstein was elected to the NAS as a foreign associate in 1922, and he was able to finally become a member after he became fully naturalized as a U.S. citizen.

The group encompasses a wide array of scientific fields. Chemistry, physics, and biology are of course included, as are geology, mathematics, psychology, and much more. Today, members outnumber foreign associates by about six to one. Einstein's election as a member was symbolic of his acceptance into the American scientific community.

In terms of humanitarian efforts, Einstein's involvement went beyond helping found the IRC. In 1925, Einstein became the first president of the World Union of Jewish Students. This organization was founded by a Jewish man from Austria, Zvi Lauterpacht. It came about because, in some European countries, there were quotas for how many Jewish people could attend the university. The match up with Einstein was obvious. Einstein was particularly concerned about Jewish education, as well as about fighting anti-Semitism in all its forms. Einstein was involved in these and similar projects during their inception, and he truly had a huge range of influence across a variety of Jewish causes and organizations.

After World War II, in 1946, Einstein became president of the Emergency Committee of Atomic Scientists. The goal of this group was to increase public awareness of the atomic bomb's potential in peacetime, and about how atomic energy could and should be used for peacetime activity. They also focused on the immorality of using atomic power for weapons. Einstein cofounded this group with his friend and previous collaborator Leo Szilard.

Einstein actually inspired famed scientist Linus Pauling (1901–1994) to join this group in 1946. Unlike most of his friends and scientific colleagues, Pauling was born in the United States. His main contribution to the scientific community came in the form of his work with protein structures, as well as the description of chemical bonds. He performed groundbreaking research into the causes of sickle-cell anemia, and he is the only person to have won two Nobel Prizes (chemistry in 1954 and peace in 1962) by himself. Needless to say, his contributions to the Emergency Committee were critical in spreading their message of how peace and technology could be compatible.

83. EINSTEIN'S OTHER PATENTS: THE COMPASS

Einstein's legacy has predominately been about his research and theories, but as we've seen, his life was much more complex than that. In addition to all the numerous other roles we've already talked about, Einstein was also an inventor. He wasn't the kind of inventor to ponder, think, and never actually create anything, either. In addition to his many "thought-experiments," he designed and actually built a number of useful items. He took cues from his former job in the patent office and actually patented many of his inventions. History is glad that Einstein went to the extra effort of protecting his inventions, because it allows historians to be aware of and study his designs. One of these many inventions was a compass.

As the story goes, when Einstein was a small child, his father showed him something he had never seen before—a pocket compass. Einstein spent quite some time trying to figure out the scientific principles behind its operation. He was fascinated by the invisible force that guided the compass and felt compelled to understand its mystery. The simple object seems to have spurred a lifetime sense of scientific curiosity on Einstein's part. It makes sense, therefore, that Einstein would return to the compass for one of his later scientific inventions.

The young Albert was given a magnetic variety, but there are actually two main types of compasses—magnetic compasses and gyrocompasses. Magnetic compasses have a needle (which is actually a magnet) that's balanced around a pivot point. The end of the needle labeled "North" always points north because it works with the Earth's magnetic core. This is the simple type of compass used by hikers to find their way around and is the type that Einstein was given as a child.

A gyrocompass, on the other hand, doesn't find north through a bar magnet. It uses a rapidly spinning wheel, along with friction and the rotation of the Earth, to find north. It gets its name from the gyroscope—a device that is basically a mounted, spinning wheel that can orient itself toward any direction. The law of conservation of angular momentum dictates that, in the absence of other forces, a freely spinning wheel will keep its original orientation or direction. What makes a gyrocompass work is the additional force of friction. Because it is actually not free to spin in any direction, it orients itself toward true north.

The gyrocompass is used mainly on ships. Why not just use a regular magnetic compass on a boat? There are two main reasons. First, gyrocompasses find true north (not magnetic north, the way a magnetic compass would). Also, some large ships are built mostly of metal, which can interfere with a magnetic compass. This device was first invented by a Dutchman, Martinus Gerardus van den Bos, in 1885. Later iterations were produced by a German scientist, Hermann Anschütz-Kaempfe, and an American, Elmer Sperry. Einstein developed an improved maritime gyrocompass of his own design in 1926, followed by an airplane gyrocompass in 1935.

Einstein's compass has become the subject of legend and folklore. There are a number of books about the compass story today, including several children's books. Why has this become such a popular story? The compass is a small device, easy to grasp, but with great power to instruct and guide. It's enchanting to think that the grand ideas of relativity and unified field theory could have all started with something as simple as a compass.

84. EINSTEIN'S OTHER PATENTS: THE HEARING AID

Albert Einstein was prolific in his inventions and designs. Among other things, did you know that Einstein worked on developing a hearing aid? As with all inventions, new ideas come from an understanding of old ones, and Einstein surely did his research into existing types of hearing devices.

Did Einstein himself have any known hearing problems? None that were made public at least. While he certainly didn't have to have a hearing problem to invent a hearing aid, it does pique one's curiosity a bit. Often, scientists invent a medical device to ameliorate a condition that they themselves suffer from or perhaps to provide assistance to someone in their family. Take Louis Braille, for instance; born in 1809 in France, Louis was the son of a leather-worker, and injured his eye while playing with an awl. Due to the subsequent infection, young Louis became blind. He attended the Paris Royal Institution for Blind Youth, where he learned of a method of raised-dot printing that had been started by a French soldier. Louis simplified the system into an entire alphabet, which is today known simply as Braille.

In this particular case, an inventor created a system based on a personal need. Einstein's hearing aid, as far as historians can tell, was not created with this sort of intent in mind. Perhaps he just wanted to create something to better help people—like with his refrigerator design (number 85). Or maybe he ran across something in his research that led naturally to the development of a hearing aid. It's also possible that Einstein had a relative with hearing trouble, and Einstein had the person in mind when he worked on this device.

Einstein's hearing aid was not the first one to be created. There were several precursors to the modern electric hearing aid. The earliest of these was probably a device known as the ear trumpet, a shell-like contraption that users would hold up to their ears to amplify sounds. Such a device was simply for people who had "trouble hearing," and the ear trumpet didn't address any specific type of hearing problem. Some of the earliest ear trumpets were manufactured in the 1880s by various companies in Germany, London, Philadelphia, and New York.

The first electric hearing aids were produced around the turn of the century. The Akouphone Company was established in 1899. Its founder, Miller Reese Hutchison, held a patent for an electric hearing aid that used a transmitter and a battery. The history of the battery is, in and of itself, a long and very interesting one. Thomas Edison introduced the first nickel-iron battery in the United States in 1901. Einstein's design, while not directly related to models currently in use, showed the true breadth of his interest and ability in the realm of design. Just as a tidbit of trivia, the first wearable hearing aid was patented in 1933 by A. Edwin Stephens.

85. THE REFRIGERATOR PUMP WITH SZILARD

Beginning in 1926, Einstein and his friend Leo Szilard united on a project that was completely unrelated to much of what they'd done before. Einstein and Szilard met in the early 1920s, and the two scientists collaborated on many projects over the course of their lives. Einstein even tried to get Szilard a job at the patent office. Perhaps fortunately, Szilard declined the invitation, but the two continued to create and innovate together. One of their more interesting inventions was a new type of refrigerator.

While it was fairly common for scientists to develop commercial items with consumer appeal, this refrigerator design had a particularly interesting background. The motivating factor for developing the refrigerator actually came from a news story about a German family living in Berlin. The refrigerator seal in the family's house broke, leaking toxic gases such as sulfur dioxide into their home and killing the entire family. And it wasn't just this one family—as mechanical refrigerators were becoming more popular than the old-style "ice boxes," more and more people were being exposed to these gases because there wasn't yet a refrigerant that could be used safely. Einstein set out to develop a safer, more family-friendly refrigerator that didn't have moving parts (at least, one that didn't have parts that could rupture). It's interesting how Einstein's humanitarian spirit extended even to the most mundane of kitchen appliances.

The main goal of Einstein's concept for the new design was to remove the part of the pump that had leaked in the infamous example in Berlin.

The pump was used to compress refrigerant as part of a heat pump cycle. Others had also tried to create new designs as well, notably two Swedish inventors named Baltzar von Platen and Carl Munters; they would later sell their design to the Electrolux Company.

Einstein and Szilard set out to improve upon the designs of von Platen and Munters, and they came up with their own plan for a noiseless, non-leaking refrigerator. They would come up with three main variations. The core of this refrigerator was the Einstein-Szilard pump, which was based on electromagnetism and diffusion. This pump was designed for home (non-commercial) refrigeration, and it was the first such device to dramatically improve safety by having no moving parts. Instead of dangerous gases, this new refrigerator design used harmless alcohol gas.

Some have suggested that the idea for this refrigerator pump actually began with Szilard. He used magnetic fields and coils to force the liquid metal through the pump. The major problem he ran into was corrosion. This appears to be the point in the process where Einstein was brought in. Einstein changed the fundamental methods through which the liquid metal was moved, and the team brought their designs into reality.

Once the ideas became a proven success, the Electrolux Company bought two of their designs. After years of trying, they finally sold the design for the pump itself to the General Electric Company of Germany in 1928. Einstein and Szilard would eventually hold eight major patents together. In total, they held forty-five patents for three different models of the home refrigeration unit. Although future innovations would send the field of refrigerator development in a different direction, away from the Einstein–Szilard design, their work certainly made an impact.

86. Einstein's later awards and honors

Rewards and accolades followed Einstein's work, especially later in his life and career. Being recognized for his achievements in this way reassured the rest of the world of the validity of Einstein's findings. Perhaps the most famous recognition was the Nobel Prize in physics in 1921, which was awarded for his research on the photoelectric effect.

The Nobel Prize was not the only formal acknowledgement of Einstein's work, though. He was awarded medals from several other institutions. In 1925, he won the Copley Medal from the Royal Society of London. This organization was started in the mid–seventeenth century by a group of scientists who wanted to share their experimental research. Founding members included such famous scientists as Robert Hooke, Christopher Wren, and Robert Boyle. The Copley Medal is the highest award given by the Royal Society, and it was received in later years by Niels Bohr and Max Planck.

Einstein went on to receive the Gold Medal from the Royal Astronomical Society in 1926. The Royal Astronomical Society is England's primary group of astronomers, geophysicists, and planetary scientists. It was begun in 1820 and was originally established to promote the relatively new sciences of astronomy and geology. Today the group houses an immense library and produces some of the scientific community's more respected publications. Other famous winners of the prestigious Gold Medal include Charles Babbage, Henri Poincaré, and Edwin Hubble.

In 1935, Einstein earned another award from a well-known institution. He won the Franklin Medal from the Franklin Institute, a unique organization dedicated to one of Einstein's lifelong goals—learning. Primarily established to celebrate achievement in science and technology, the Franklin Center's mission includes informing and educating the public about advances in the sciences. The awards program was begun in 1832 as a way to encourage scientific invention and discovery. Einstein's particular award was given for his work with both relativity and the photoelectric effect.

It is easy to recognize Albert Einstein as one of the most important people to have lived in the last century. In numerous arenas such as science, politics, and religion, he was truly a singular individual. Yet not everyone who has wished to honor him has been willing to accept all aspects of Einstein's life.

In July 2002, Israel canceled an Albert Einstein exhibit they had sponsored that was planned to be on display in China during the month of September. The exhibit had been scheduled to premiere in Beijing, and then travel to Shanghai and other Chinese cities, lasting four months in total.

The exhibit was ultimately cancelled because the Chinese Ministry of Culture wanted to remove all references to Einstein's Judaism. Especially in the later part of his life, Einstein and his identity with the Jewish people were inseparable. To remove this aspect of his life would have been telling only part of the story behind whom he was and why he made the decisions he did.

Part 6

FUTURE IMPACT AND INFLUENCE

As we've seen, Einstein's work has had far-reaching effects on modern society. And there remains more. As we begin our trek into the twenty-first century, Einstein's legacy is still with us, alive and very well.

Einstein's work on relativity is one of the things that allows us to have a global positioning system (GPS). Only recently have organizations such as the National Space and Aeronautics Administration (NASA) been able to put certain theories and ideas to the test, technology finally being able to provide some amazing answers to the questions he discovered decades before.

Beyond the concrete scientific aspects, Einstein's legacy has become a cultural one. So powerful is the figure he cuts in modern society that he has become the blueprint for what we now call genius.

87. Test of general relativity: Gravity Probe B

One of the biggest tests of Einstein's theory of general relativity is finally taking place after decades of study. The Gravity Probe B spacecraft, developed by NASA and Stanford University, was launched in April 2004 after forty years of development and experimentation. The spacecraft contains four extremely accurate gyroscopes, and the experiment will make precise measurements of any changes in their spin as the spacecraft orbits the Earth in a polar orbit. Gravity Probe B will allow scientists to finally test two predictions of Einstein's theory of general relativity that have yet to be confirmed.

The gyroscopes on Gravity Probe B were designed to be free of other disturbances, and so can provide a space-time reference system that is almost perfect. The experiment will therefore be able to measure how space and time themselves are warped by the presence of the Earth. It can also determine how the rotation of the Earth actually drags space-time with it.

When Einstein proposed his theory of general relativity in 1916, the groundbreaking theory was of course immensely controversial. It didn't help that the theory was also extremely difficult to test thoroughly. Einstein came up with a few different ways to test it, but all pushed the limits of instrumentation at the time and could also be explained by other models. These effects included the precession of the perihelion of Mercury, the deflection of starlight, and the gravitational redshift.

It was only in the 1960s that technology had progressed sufficiently to make sophisticated tests that could support general relativity and rule out competing theories. One example of such a program is NASA's Gravity Probe A, which confirmed the gravitational redshift prediction. Still, important predictions of general relativity remained untested. One of these is called "frame dragging"—this is an effect where a large massive body that is rotating should actually drag space and time around with it. The effect is small, but it was predicted in the 1960s that an orbiting gyroscope should be able to detect it, if the gyroscope were sufficiently precise. Another effect, called the geodetic effect, measures the actual curvature of space-time caused by the presence of the Earth. Again, this can be detected by an orbiting gyroscope. Unfortunately for physicists, it took forty years before a sufficiently accurate gyroscope could be built and flown on a spacecraft to make these measurements.

The measurements and results from Gravity Probe B, expected in 2005 and 2006, will have very important implications for the applicability of general relativity to the structure of the universe as a whole. It will also have impact on the nature of matter itself. Scientists have made predictions about the measurements they think Gravity Probe B will make, but the results could either support general relativity, or potentially even rule it out. While the effects expected to be measured at the Earth will be extremely small, when extrapolated up to the scale of a galaxy they could be huge indeed, as could their implications.

88. Bose-Einstein condensates

Einstein's work had a tendency to have an impact far beyond its initial area of research. In the study of subzero temperatures, Einstein's predictions found yet another application that was outside the original realm of intention. This particular case involves Satyendra Nath Bose (1894–1974) an Indian physicist who studied how light was transmitted in small packets called "quanta." Einstein took this idea and applied it to atoms, but he found that strange things happened when atoms were exposed to extremely low temperatures.

Einstein had first encountered Bose scientifically in 1924, when Einstein received a paper by Bose that had initially been rejected for publication. When Einstein received the paper from Bose, he immediately realized its importance and pushed to get it published. In his paper, Bose proposed that photons could exist in different states, and that the number of photons was not conserved. This observation led to the property of photons called "spin". Einstein also reviewed a later paper from Bose on the subject of treating photons as consisting of a gas made up of identical particles. This assumption allowed Bose to derive a law for blackbody radiation. Einstein took Bose's theory a step further, though. He used Bose's calculations to predict that matter would enter a new phase when it reached absolute zero. At this point, atoms would become part of an ideal system, where their quantum and mechanical properties would equal out.

At this level, Einstein predicted that a special kind of condensation would form. At this lowest of possible temperatures, atoms would join together to act as a single entity. This particular phenomenon has been dubbed "Bose-Einstein condensation," or BEC. Einstein also showed that this particular condensation only applied to particles called "bosons"— ones with a particular relationship between spin and Planck's constant.

The discovery of a new phase of matter was incredibly significant, since, at that time, it was believed that matter could exist only in one of four phases (solid, liquid, gas, and plasma). This new phase was dubbed the "Bose-Einstein condensate." One of the results of this prediction was that quantum physics could be examined on a larger scale, since larger groups of atoms could now be studied as representatives of their smaller, constituent atoms.

Scientists and others tried for years to create Bose-Einstein condensation in a laboratory. They were initially met with failure, but perseverance ultimately paid off. The prediction of this new phase of matter was eventually proven in 1995, when a team of scientists actually created a Bose-Einstein condensate. A team of scientists led by Eric Cornell and Carl Wieman working at the Joint Institute for Laboratory Astrophysics (JILA) in Boulder, Colorado, as well as Wolfgang Ketterle of MIT, conducted this research, and they shared the 2001 Nobel Prize in physics for their work.

89. Einstein's Dreams of World Government and Peace

One of Einstein's lifelong goals was to see the creation of a world government. Rather than individual states and countries having their own separate institutions of power, he favored the idea of a worldwide organization that could be devoted to solving conflicts and problems peacefully, without war. While pride in oneself was something Einstein was a strong proponent of, he was not overly fond of extreme patriotism. Remember that Einstein lived through Nazi Germany and saw first-hand the dangers of too much pride in one's country. Einstein, it was known, was true to the human race, not any particular nation, perhaps the ultimate expression of a humanitarian.

For this reason, Einstein was a primary player in the World Government Movement. It was an attempt to create a coalition with these exact motives—to remove national boundaries as much as possible, and live in a one-world environment. The movement actually stemmed from the *One World or None Report* of 1946, subtitled "A Report to the Public on the Full Meaning of the Atomic Bomb." While it focused on how to prevent an arms race by not letting individual countries control such devastating weapons individually, the basic principles were right in line with Einstein's understanding of world peace.

The main problem Einstein saw with localized governments was represented in the fear and insecurity that he witnessed in McCarthy-era America. Individual governments, he thought, would need to assume that war might erupt at some point, hence the need for military buildup. Similarly, individual families felt a constant need to defend themselves, always feeling threatened by an unknown (or, in some cases, known) attacker. This sense of impending doom led to fear, which in turn led to violence. Einstein described this situation as a vicious circle, one that he felt humanity needed to break away from.

Given these assumptions, he presented two choices: either be prepared for war or create a worldwide government so that war would not be necessary. He saw the General Assembly of the United Nations (UN) as a step in the right direction, but one that was insufficient by itself. The UN, founded in 1942, had, in its short existence during Einstein's lifetime, failed to prevent war. It could not be held completely responsible, however, because Einstein understood that no single organization could be any stronger than its constituent parts. In the case of the individual countries of the UN, these composite parts were heading toward war, rendering the larger group helpless to stop it.

Einstein's search for a unified theory in physics ran parallel with his wish for global peace and a unified world government where people treated other people humanely and sensibly. He spent his life working toward both of these goals: the unity of science and of humanity. While he did not reach either, it can be argued that he made the world a better place on both fronts just through his efforts.

Einstein's humanitarianism followed him almost literally to the grave. His final project, which he worked on at the hospital, was a speech marking Israel's seventh Independence Day. In it, he wrote about the conflict between Israel and Egypt, mentioning the tendency leaders have to twist reality according to their own perceptions. Einstein noted that while much of the world considered the conflict a minor matter, there should actually be no distinction between large and small problems. Until truth and justice were served, no problem was too small to be heard.

90. EINSTEIN'S WORK AS PRECURSOR FOR GPS

Have you ever ridden in a car with a voice interactive global positioning system (GPS) in it? Ever eye the handheld GPS units for sale in trendy tech shops and wonder if your neighborhood has been mapped for all the world to see? Been lost in a strange neighborhood, or out hiking in the wilderness, and found it handy to refer to your computerized map system for a way out? Well, you can thank Albert Einstein for helping make all that possible.

General relativity led to a number of scientific breakthroughs and theoretical changes, but it also made its way down to personal technology that affects people in their everyday lives. One "side effect" of relativity is the idea that time passes at different rates depending on your altitude. This effect had to be taken into account when GPS systems were designed.

Global positioning systems work by receiving signals from satellites in orbit around Earth. Each of these satellites has an atomic clock, so that it is always using the correct time. Multiple satellites transmit signals, and there's a time delay due to the fact that signals are emitted at intervals.

These signals are encoded so that the GPS device (usually a handheld unit, or one inserted into an automobile, airplane, or other means of transportation) knows exactly where the satellite was (and how it was positioned) at the time the signal was emitted. The speed of light is used to translate the time delays between satellites into distances, and the GPS system figures out exactly where it is at any given time.

To accurately determine a position on the ground, the clocks on GPS satellites must run with an accuracy of 1 nanosecond (1 billionth of a second). However, the satellites are moving with respect to observers on the ground. So both special and general relativity must be taken into account. The designers of GPS satellites must account for both the time dilation from special relativity, and the fact that time moves at different rates depending on altitude, from general relativity.

When the first test GPS satellite was put into orbit in 1977, the scientists were a bit dubious that the general relativity correction was necessary. They left it out of the main clock, but they put in a special module that could be activated to perform the correction if necessary (just in case Einstein was right after all). Sure enough, after three weeks, the time on the satellite clock differed from a clock on the ground by just the amount predicted by Einstein. The scientists turned on the module and left it on.

Overall, then, thanks to Einstein, relativistic effects can be calculated exactly and built into the clocks on the GPS satellites. Without the relativistic corrections, the GPS satellites would fall out of synch within minutes, and positional errors on the ground would start to build up by about ten kilometers every day. Without Einstein's theory of relativity, GPS positioning would not be possible. Hikers would have a lot more trouble finding their way around the mountains, and airplanes wouldn't have GPS trackers in the cockpit to guide the pilot (and everyone else on board) back down to the ground.

91. EINSTEIN IN POPULAR MEDIA

One of the major ways in which the public is made aware of advances in all fields is through the media. Newspapers, books, television, and film help "spread the word" concerning just about every aspect of modern society. In Einstein's case, aside from relaying information about his scientific advances, the media has adapted Einstein's name and character in a variety of public-interest situations that have tremendously increased people's general awareness of Albert Einstein.

One of the first popular films to capitalize on Einstein was a comedy film from 1988 entitled *Young Einstein*. In this movie, which is sometimes billed as an "alternative biography," Einstein's inventions (both real and some fictionalized ones) are described and his contribution to history is explained. This movie takes more than a few liberties with his life—Einstein is credited with, among other things, splitting the "beer molecule" and inventing rock and roll. The movie *Young Einstein* was directed by an actor/director named Yahoo Serious. While Einstein was known for having a good sense of humor, the liberties taken by this film might have gone a bit too far.

Einstein's popular influence extended into literature as well. *Einstein's Dreams*, a book by Alan Lightman, discusses Einstein's place in history

$\Sigma\theta'\frac{\lambda}{\pi\Delta}\lambda$ $\frac{\alpha}{\pi\theta}$ $"\pi\theta\Delta\Sigma\theta'\frac{\lambda}{\pi\Delta}\lambda$ $\frac{\alpha}{\pi\theta}\frac{\sigma}{\Delta\pi}\chi\Delta\pi\Sigma\theta\frac{\alpha}{\pi\Delta}\lambda$ $\frac{\alpha}{\pi\theta}\frac{\sigma}{\Delta\pi}\chi\Delta\pi\theta\Delta$ α

accurately, then delves into the unknown with thirty discussions of some of Einstein's most salient theoretical quests. Many largely nonfictional books have also been written about Einstein's personal life. Some of the more prominent include *Einstein in Love: A Scientific Romance* by Dennis Overbye and *Einstein's Daughter: The Search for Liesel* by Michele Zackheim. There is no lack of interest in the life of one of history's greatest scientists, that's for sure.

And that interest even extends into children's literature. A popular children's book called *Rescuing Einstein's Compass* has Albert going for a sail with the child of a friend. Einstein drops his precious compass, which is retrieved by the child, and the book teaches how every person has their own way of contributing to someone else's happiness. This recent classic by Shulamith Levey Oppenheim is a great, fun way to introduce young children to Einstein, invention, and curiosity.

Another important way in which Einstein influenced the course of literature was that his scientific concepts found translation into the world of poetry. The fact that Einstein's research led to a denial of "absolute time" entered the world of writing; authors began portraying time as dynamic, in flux, and never static. An example of this new sort of writing can be seen in the work of William Faulkner's *The Sound and the Fury*, one of the first books that told a story from multiple perspectives, rather than from the voice of a single narrator located at a single point in time. Similarly, the field of objectivist poetry came into light with the works of poets such as Archibald MacLeish, who produced works like *End of the World* and *Ars Poetica* that experimented with new forms of meter and literary structure.

92. Schwarzschild using Einstein's Results for Black Holes

Black holes were first studied by German astronomer Karl Schwarzschild (1873–1916) in 1916. In solving Einstein's equations of general relativity for a perfectly spherical, nonrotating object, Schwarzschild showed that a sufficiently massive object would result in an infinite curvature of space-time, meaning that light would not only be bent, it could not escape at all.

Einstein reported on Schwarzschild's results at a meeting, but Einstein himself never believed that such an object could exist in reality. Rather, Einstein considered them to be bizarre mathematical constructs. The term "black hole" was coined after Einstein's death, and since the 1960s, there has been increasing evidence that these bizarre features could indeed exist in our universe.

One possible way that a black hole might be formed is at the end of the life of a large star. Such a star could gravitationally collapse on itself, and if it had sufficient mass to begin with, it could reach a point of critical density and form a black hole. But how could such objects be detected?

General relativity, which predicts the existence of black holes, also contains a possible method for detecting them. Einstein's theory suggests that disturbances in space-time produce gravitational waves. These waves are produced by the oscillation of the fabric of space-time itself. Gravity waves were a controversial suggestion, and many were skeptical when they were first suggested.

$$\Sigma\theta'\frac{i}{\pi\lambda}\,\frac{\sigma}{\pi}\theta \qquad \sqrt[\alpha]{\pi}\,\theta_\Delta\Sigma\theta'\frac{i}{\pi\lambda}\,\frac{\sigma}{\pi}\theta_\Delta\frac{\sigma}{\pi}\pi^\chi\Delta^\pi\Sigma\theta\,\sqrt[\alpha]{\pi\lambda}\,\frac{\sigma}{\pi}\theta_\Delta\frac{\sigma}{\pi}\pi^\chi\Delta^\pi\theta_\Delta^{\alpha}$$

However, recently scientists have found a number of ways to show the possible existence of gravitational waves. First, a binary pulsar system was shown to have a decrease in its orbital period, which is the exact amount that would be suggested if it were giving off gravitational waves and thus losing energy. In the future, a number of experiments are planned to search for gravitational waves directly, including the Laser Interferometer Gravitational-Wave Observatory (LIGO).

93. WHY EINSTEIN'S GREATEST BLUNDER MIGHT ACTUALLY HAVE BEEN RIGHT

As Einstein developed his theory of general relativity, he faced a problem. Einstein's theories predicted that the universe was expanding, a fact which originally Einstein did not believe until astronomical evidence was found. To counter the expansion, Einstein posited that even the emptiest of space still had its own inherent dark energy, which he called the cosmological constant. He used this result to balance out the expansion that his equations called for to keep the universe static. When the expansion of the universe was later discovered, Einstein called the cosmological constant his greatest blunder. Yet we now know that the expansion of the universe is actually accelerating, and dark energy could be the cause. But we do not understand the nature of dark energy, where it comes from, how it acts, or even what it is.

Einstein's theories originally predicted an expanding universe, but in the 1990s, it was discovered that this expansion was actually accelerating, speeding up over time. The source of this acceleration seems to come from a strange force that acts to oppose gravity, called dark energy. Dark energy, which had also been suggested from quantum theory, is now thought to dominate the mass-energy makeup of the entire universe. This bizarre form of energy would actually exist throughout empty space, taking up much of the volume of the universe. Little is known about dark energy's strange properties, but scientists suspect that its repulsive properties are what is causing the expansion of the universe to accelerate, as the universe literally pulls itself apart.

The cosmological constant, as it has now been revived, actually comes from quantum mechanics, the study of physics at the smallest possible scales. The ties between the cosmological study of galaxies and the quantum study of subatomic particles may seem ephemeral, but they are important in today's theories of physics. The cosmological constant has come to represent a strange kind of energy density that remains constant as the universe expands, and which has a repulsive gravitational force rather than the standard attractive gravitational force. The laws of quantum physics say that such a configuration can only exist in empty space, but in the strange world of quantum mechanics even empty space is not really empty—it is full of pairs of virtual particles that appear and disappear. These particles give even empty space its own fundamental energy. And observations that show that the expansion of the universe is actually accelerating require a much higher energy density than is seen in the observable universe. This strange vacuum energy, also called dark energy, could account for the extra 70 percent required to make the universe's expansion accelerate.

A future NASA mission has been proposed to measure the expansion accurately enough to determine whether dark energy is a constant attribute of empty space, as Einstein proposed, or whether it shows signs of any structure, which would be consistent with modern unified theories of physics. In a bizarre twist, it might just turn out one day that what Einstein considered his greatest blunder (the cosmological constant) and the part of physics he believed in the least (quantum physics) could be combined to help develop a unified theory of space, time, gravity, and quantum physics. The unsuccessful search for just such a grand unified theory occupied much of Einstein's career.

94. EINSTEIN AND THE IMAGE OF GENIUS: WHAT HE LOOKED LIKE IN 1905 COMPARED WITH LATER IN HIS LIFE

What do you think of when picturing a brilliant scientific mind? The stereotypical image of a flailing scientist with wild, unkempt hair, a sense of fashion that would be considered challenged even in the most generous estimation and, of course, a general aura of being just a bit off? Such a description may superficially fit not only the majority of the images of scientists in modern media, but certainly bears more than a passing resemblance to Albert Einstein in his later years.

Of course, what history often chooses to forget is that when he was actually developing his theories of relativity, Einstein appeared much more "normal looking" and less what we have come to think of as eccentric-looking. During his years at the Swiss patent office, Einstein wore a traditional suit and tie to work, and his hair was of a more normal length. Being younger, of course, his hair was much less white as well. Only well after his 1905 series of groundbreaking papers did Einstein's appearance begin to shift. It has to be asked: Was the eccentric behavior always a part of who Einstein was from the beginning of his life? Or was the distinctive look he became known for merely a byproduct of his success? Being well known certainly came with some significant advantages; he was allowed to focus on his work, putting aside all the normal concerns and conventions that plague everyday people. It would certainly make sense that his continued success and recognition allowed Einstein to ignore certain social conventions—like wearing socks.

95. Baby Einstein

Using Einstein as the prototype for a certain type of genius as portrayed in popular media and literature is almost a cliché. Amusingly, Einstein has also invaded popular culture beyond normal entertainment—his face is commonly invoked as the face of genius, and his face adorns T-shirts, coffee mugs, and other commercial items. What would the modest patent clerk have thought of this kind of fame?

One of the main benefits of Einstein's personal fame is that it brought science into public view. Through the cult of his personality, Einstein was able to gain public recognition of some rather obscure breakthroughs in various areas of physics. Few other scientists have been able to get the public to listen to their theories at all, let alone have them enter popular discussions in ways such as "everything's relative." And Einstein believed firmly in educating the masses; if the use of his name convinced a few more young people to want to study science, he probably would have come out in favor of the idea.

Today, Einstein's name is present in society in ways both scientific and silly. The element einsteinium was named after him, in recognition of his many contributions to atomic science. A line of baby products, called "Baby Einstein," claims to be able to increase the intelligence of your infant. Capitalizing on the popular correlation of the name Einstein with genius, these products include videotapes, audio recordings, and other items—none of which have anything to do with Einstein. They attempt to provide an educational experience for your child that might help turn her into the next Einstein. Of course, none of this has been proven scientifically, but that doesn't stop legions of parents from purchasing them, eager to give their children any edge possible. As a marketing mantra, it's hard to go wrong with "Be like Einstein."

96. EINSTEIN COLLEGE OF MEDICINE AND OTHER TRIBUTES

As yet another testament to the profound effect Einstein had on the world, a number of scholarships, monuments, foundations, and other functions have been dedicated in honor of one of history's greatest scientists. There are far too many to list each one individually. However, looking at a few highlights gives an idea of how far-reaching this aspect of his influence has been.

One of the most well known fellowships to bear Einstein's name is the Albert Einstein Distinguished Educator Fellowship. It provides educational fellowships in math and science for teachers at both the elementary and secondary school levels. This program is administered by the U.S. Department of Energy, and it lets teachers who win the award spend time in either a Congressional office or a federal agency (such as the National Science Foundation or NASA). The winners of this award are primarily responsible for helping to shape the path that math and science education in America takes, and, as such, they contribute enormously to developing the minds of the next generation of future scientists.

One of many visible tributes to Albert Einstein can be seen in the Albert Einstein Memorial Statue, located in conjunction with the National Academy of Sciences building in Washington, D.C. This statue, created by artist Robert Berks, was unveiled in 1979 to commemorate the 100-year anniversary of Einstein's birth. This bronze work of art shows Einstein holding papers that discuss his most important contributions to science—general relativity, the photoelectric effect, and $E = mc^2$.

Although not built as a monument to Einstein, Yeshiva University in New York City bears the Einstein name in a very tangible form. Yeshiva University, founded in 1886, honors the great scientist through its Albert Einstein College of Medicine. The school first opened in 1955, and Einstein gave his approval to the name shortly before that. Yeshiva University also offers an Albert Einstein Award; Harry Belafonte is one famous recipient.

Various other organizations and societies offer Albert Einstein awards. Usually they are for either academic merit, achievements in the sciences, or civil service. One of many examples is the Albert Einstein Technology Medal, given by the State of Israel. The purpose of this award is to recognize individuals who make significant creative contributions in the technology industry. Recipients of this prize have included Margaret Thatcher and Steven Spielberg. Another is the Albert Einstein Award, given by a Jewish institution called the American Society of Technion.

It is almost impossible to go through life not knowing who Einstein was. While his discoveries certainly were capable of standing on their own, a large part of the reason we all know his name is that it has been recycled so often through the media. Incredible intelligence coupled with a successful (though unintended) marketing campaign served to bring Einstein's name to the forefront, thereby allowing his immense legacy to continue growing.

97. Einsteinium

Einstein's legacy appears in the periodic table as well. Einsteinium (symbol Es, atomic number 99) was discovered in 1952 as a byproduct of the first hydrogen bomb explosion. It was discovered in Berkeley, California, by a team of scientists led by Albert Ghiorso. Also aiding in the discovery was a team lead by G. R. Choppin, who worked as Los Alamos National Laboratory. Both teams had been studying the debris left over from

$\Sigma \theta^{i} \pi \lambda \; \frac{\alpha}{\theta} \Delta_{\pi}^{\sigma} \; \chi \Delta \pi \; \theta_{\Delta} \Sigma \theta^{i} \pi \lambda \; \frac{\alpha}{\theta} \Delta_{\pi}^{\sigma} \chi \Delta \pi \Sigma \theta \; \pi \lambda \; \frac{\alpha}{\theta} \Delta_{\pi}^{\sigma} \chi \Delta \pi \theta_{\Delta}$

hydrogen bomb testing and realized that a new isotope (einsteinium) was created by nuclear fusion. They decided to name it einsteinium in recognition to Einstein's fundamental research that led to the development of the bomb.

The actual isotope the team uncovered, called einsteinium–253, has a half-life of twenty days. It is a synthetic element and a very radioactive one at that. It can be produced in a laboratory, and in 1961, scientists made about .01 mg of einsteinium—they used it to create another element, mendelevium. The Oak Ridge National Laboratory, located in Tennessee, also made about 3 mg of this element, which as you can imagine is not an easy task. The scientists there had to irradiate large amounts of plutonium in a reactor, a process that took several years. They then had to make plutonium oxide pellets and aluminum powder from the resulting material and placed the pellets into target rods. These rods were then irradiated for an additional year before being placed in a high flux isotopic reactor (HRIF) for four more months. As you can see, einsteinium isn't one of those things that you're likely to find in a chemistry set.

Ultimately, seventeen radioisotopes of einsteinium would be discovered, with varying degrees of stability. Einsteinium–252 (Es–252) was the most stable, as it had a half-life of 471.7 days. Some of the radioactive isotopes had half-lives as short as a few hours or minutes.

Chemically, einsteinium is the seventh metallic transuranic element and is made by assaulting plutonium with multiple neutrons. Its chemical properties are similar to other heavy actinide elements (the "actinide series" on the periodic table refers to the fourteen elements in between actinium and nobelium). It produces radiation, but einsteinium has yet to be found to serve any practical purpose.

Einsteinium has the following characteristics:

- *Element symbol*: Es
- *Atomic number*: 99
- *Atomic mass*: 254
- *Room temperature state*: Solid
- *Melting point*: 860 degrees Kelvin
- *Group*: rare Earth, Actinides
- *Electronegativity*: 1.3
- *Electron affinity*: 50 kJ/mol

Einstein, of course, was not the only famous scientist to have an element of the periodic table named after him. To name just a few, Bohrium (Bh, 107) is named for Niels Bohr, fermium (Fm, 100) is named after Enrico Fermi, and mendelevium (Md, 101) corresponds to Dmitri Mendeleyev.

98. Einstein: Person of the Century

Einstein's impact on society clearly goes beyond coffee mugs and T-shirts. One of the all-time great honors bestowed upon Einstein was given by Time magazine, when it announced Albert Einstein as the Person of the

$\Sigma\theta^{\ddot{a}}_{\pi\lambda}\lambda\ ^{\alpha}\mathring{\theta}\triangle^{\sigma}_{\Sigma\pi}\chi\ddot{\Delta}^{\prime\prime}\pi\theta\triangle\Sigma\theta^{\ddot{a}}_{\pi\lambda}\lambda\ ^{\alpha}\mathring{\theta}\triangle^{\sigma}_{\Sigma\pi}\chi\ddot{\Delta}^{\prime\prime}\pi\Sigma\theta^{u}_{\pi\lambda}\lambda\ ^{\alpha}\mathring{\theta}\triangle^{\sigma}_{\Sigma\pi}\chi\ddot{\Delta}^{\prime\prime}\pi\theta\triangle^{u}$

Century in 2000. This honor served to awaken interest in history's greatest scientist and, as a result, in science itself.

In earning this most prestigious honor, Einstein beat out two of the twentieth century's most important figures, both of whom were his contemporaries. Franklin Delano Roosevelt (FDR) was one of the top runners-up who lost this award to Albert Einstein. FDR (1882–1945) was elected president of the United States in 1932. He was already a skilled politician and one who had gained the respect of both his peers and the general public. He was elected during the midst of the Great Depression. FDR connected directly with the people via his "fireside chats," introduced New Deal legislation to help the economy recover from the Depression, and was re-elected president in 1936 and 1940. He led the country in World War II, and FDR interacted with Einstein on the subject of atomic development. Franklin Roosevelt's impact on the country's economy, involvement in the war, and development of atomic and nuclear weapons was monumental.

The other runner-up for the Person of the Century Award was Mohandas Gandhi (1869–1948). Gandhi was an activist from India, who worked most of his life toward achieving nonviolent, peaceful unification of the Indian state. After living in London and South Africa for a number of years, he returned to India to commit himself fully to helping his native country. His main goal was lifting India from under British rule, but he wanted to do so through love and peaceful noncooperation, not violence. His commitment to his cause was truly extraordinary, and India was granted independence in 1947 (a year before Gandhi was assassinated).

One thing to keep in mind about *Time*'s selection process for awards such as this (i.e., their annual Person of the Year Award) is how they select their winners. One of the main criteria is the level of impact that a person has on a global scale in a given time period. That is why in varying years, such awards have been bestowed upon Adolf Hitler, Winston Churchill, and Martin Luther King Jr. It isn't always about popularity or recognition; rather it is about impact upon the world we live in as a whole. Albert Einstein changed the entire course of scientific discovery; a more potent figure is hard to imagine.

It was, then, no small achievement for Einstein to have won this award. He was chosen over candidates who were incredibly influential in their fields and who made their own indelible marks on history. The fact that Einstein won proves how large an influence he had and over what a wide-reaching area. *Time*'s citation mentions Einstein's contributions to many different parts of society over the many years of his influence. As the most recognized scientist of a century that could very well be dubbed the "century for science," he was an obvious choice.

99. EINSTEIN ON THE BEACH: A GENIUS IN POPULAR MEDIA

Einstein's influence on popular culture extended into the realm of music as well. Philip Glass (born in 1937) is a modern American composer who began learning the violin at age six and flute at age eight. He studied mathematics and philosophy in college, later excelling at Juilliard in New York. During

$\Sigma\theta\dot{m}\lambda \quad {}^{\alpha}\dot{\eta}\theta_4\frac{\sigma}{\pi} \quad \chi\ddot{\Delta}\pi\theta_\Delta\Sigma\theta\dot{m}\lambda \quad {}^{\alpha}\dot{\eta}\theta_4\frac{\sigma}{\pi}\chi\ddot{\Delta}\pi\Sigma\theta\overset{\alpha}{m}\lambda \quad {}^{\alpha}\dot{\eta}\theta_4\frac{\sigma}{\pi}\chi\ddot{\Delta}\pi\theta_\Delta \overset{\alpha}{}$

that period Glass studied American composers such as William Schuman and Aaron Copeland; he later lived and worked in Paris under the tutelage of composer, conductor, and teacher, Nadia Boulanger. There, he became intimately familiar with the work of legendary sitar virtuoso Ravi Shankar and soon became entrenched in Eastern musical technique.

Glass co-founded a theater company, Mabou Mines, and also started his own performing group called the Philip Glass Ensemble. He composed numerous music-theater pieces during this part of his life, including *Music in 12 Parts*, *Satyagraha*, and *Einstein on the Beach*.

Glass produced the music and lyrics to *Einstein on the Beach*, a modern four-act opera that created an entirely new type of musical piece. This work was first produced in 1976. A five-hour-long production (without intermissions), *Einstein* was designed as an opera in four acts, with roles for chorus, ensemble, and solo performers. Philip Glass provided the music and lyrics, while Robert Wilson was the designer and director. The opera vaulted Glass and Wilson to fame.

The opera itself consists of a series of "knee play" interludes that alternated with the text of the story; these knee plays also provided time for scenery changes. This new style of composition and presentation changed the face of Western music. The sparse ensemble includes violin, flute, saxophone, and keyboard, all played by a group of just five musicians, while the chorus contains the full range of vocals (soprano, mezzo-soprano, tenor, and baritone). There is also spoken text throughout the production.

Glass gave this piece its name because Einstein was one of his childhood heroes; growing up with the aftermath of World War II, Glass wrote, it was next to impossible to be unaware of who Einstein was and what his impact on the world had been. The coming of the nuclear age was an unavoidable topic of discussion during Glass's formative years, especially with the impact of the atomic bomb. Einstein's association with these events, however minimal, left an impact on Glass. His opera was intended to examine all aspects of Einstein—physicist, musician, and humanitarian. Glass described *Einstein on the Beach* as "an opera about a great mathematician who loved music".

Einstein on the Beach was a groundbreaking piece of musical theater, breaking all the rules and tacitly giving permission for other experimental work that followed. It has no plot, although there are many references to Einstein throughout the piece. The opera takes a metaphorical look at Einstein's life and his role in the splitting of the atom, considering him (inaccurately) as the "father of the bomb". The work is constructed of a series of minimalist musical structures, repeated in a mathematical method with various permutations throughout the opera, while a chorus chants a series of numbers. The final scene of the work is an abstract representation of the aftermath of a nuclear explosion, building to an anxious finale full of pulsing repetitive musical accompaniment and frenzied choral chants.

Einstein on the Beach was perhaps the peak of Glass's modernist and minimalist work, breaking all the rules in an unprecedented fashion. While it originally opened to mixed reviews, over the years it has been recognized as a work almost without precedent, and it has been revived numerous times and has had an enormous impact on modern theater. Glass's later works almost seem conventional, when compared to *Einstein on the Beach.*

100. How was Einstein a genius? Definition of a genius

Albert Einstein was, to be sure, one of the world's all-time great minds. He was considered a genius by his peers, and history has certainly remembered him as such. What exactly does one have to do in order to be considered a genius? How do Einstein's achievements compare to those of other people that history has also dubbed "genius"?

What makes a genius?

The history of the world is generally thought of in one of several ways. It can be conceived of as a smattering of events; for example, World War I is a defining feature in any world history book. History can also be seen as a series of inventions. The development of steel, the automobile, and baseball were certainly key inventions that influence many aspects of modern life.

Alternatively, world history can be seen in terms of those who have shaped it—the great minds, "geniuses"—who contributed significantly toward providing a force strong enough to change the world and create history. What makes someone a genius? What does someone have to do in order for history to bestow upon them this ultimate praise?

Plain old smart

Natural intelligence surely plays a major role. Not everyone in the world is capable of thinking or acting at a genius level. If they were, the world would be chock-full of geniuses. While everyone can, of course, make significant contributions to the world, it seems to take something extra to have one's name recognized far and wide and to contribute ideas and creations that withstand the test of time.

Ingenuity

Creativity is also critical toward someone becoming known as a genius. People generally become famous by inventing something new—not by re-inventing something that's already been created. While most modern inventions are based on pre-existing ideas, to a greater or lesser extent, a part of genius lies in the ability to create something new out of as little existing material as possible and to make that new invention unique. Genius, then, requires intelligence coupled with innovation.

Luck

Being in the right place at the right time is also a large factor in determining whom society will remember as a genius. Creating something necessary, right at the time when its importance is most evident, will give an inventor very favorable status. Solving what's seen to be a societal dilemma, or filling a perceived void, can lead to fame. Then again, sometimes when an invention or idea is amazing enough, its creator will be seen as a genius irrespective of his or her place in history.

101.“Beyond Einstein”

Einstein's theories of the universe revolutionized twentieth-century scientific thinking. Now, in the twenty-first century, we can begin to understand Einstein's legacy, as extensions of his work shape our current scientific mysteries. NASA has designed an ambitious scientific program called "Beyond Einstein," which attempts to examine the structure and evolution of the universe through extensions of Einstein's theories.

Einstein himself thought three major results of his work on the nature of the universe were so outlandish that they could not possibly be true. But current research suggests that, in fact, Einstein was correct in these predictions as well as in so much else of his work. These three results include the Big Bang theory of the origin of the universe; the existence of black holes; and the presence of dark energy.

Each of these three results is now suspected to be correct, but each of the results raises many unanswered questions. NASA's Beyond Einstein program aims to answer three specific questions, each an offshoot of one of the results mentioned above.

1. We now believe, based on evidence from the cosmic microwave background radiation and other clues, that the universe began with a giant explosion dubbed the Big Bang, and that the universe has been expanding steadily outward from that point in space and time, as predicted by Einstein's theories. Yet we do not know what powered the Big Bang. (See number 54.)

2. It appears that black holes, which were a mathematical result of Einstein's theories of gravity, actually exist. These are locations where the gravitational pull of a collapsed star is so strong that nothing, not even light, can escape. Yet we do not understand what happens to space, time, and matter right at the edge of a black hole, on the boundary between normal space and the bizarre world inside. (See numbers 60 and 93.)

3. Einstein's theories predicted that the universe was expanding, a fact which Einstein did not originally believe until astronomical evidence was found. To counter the expansion, Einstein suggested that even the emptiest of space still had its own inherent dark energy, which he called the cosmological constant. He used this result to balance out the expansion that his equations called for, to keep the universe static. When the expansion of the universe was later discovered, Einstein called the cosmological constant his greatest blunder. Yet we now know that the expansion of the universe is actually accelerating, and dark energy could be the cause. But we do not understand the nature of dark energy, where it comes from, how it acts, or even what it is. (See number 93.)

To answer these three questions requires that we move beyond the world of physics that even Einstein was able to study, into realms that require the most cutting-edge methods and experiments of physics and astronomy.

To study black holes, Beyond Einstein missions will study gravitational waves, a form of energy predicted by Einstein. Gravitational waves will allow us to detect activity from black holes, and study how they form, merge, and collide. These waves are extremely difficult to detect, and, in fact, Einstein never thought that gravitational waves could be detected directly. Yet today, in the twenty-first century, we have the technology to do just that. The Constellation-X mission is proposed to study black holes with high resolution x-ray spectroscopy, and the LISA mission is proposed to detect gravitational waves.

To study the Big Bang, measurements must be made that can separate out the effects of gravitons from the energy that actually powered the Big Bang. A spacecraft called an "Inflation Probe" has been proposed to study gravitational waves and their effect on the cosmic microwave background.

Einstein's theories originally predicted an expanding universe, but in the 1990s it was discovered that this expansion was actually speeding up over time. The source of this acceleration seems to come from a strange force that acts to oppose gravity, called dark energy. Dark energy, which had also been suggested from quantum theory, is now thought to dominate the mass-energy makeup of the entire universe. Little is known about dark energy's strange properties, but scientists suspect that its repulsive properties are what is causing the expansion of the universe to accelerate, as the universe literally pulls itself apart. A mission in the Beyond Einstein program will measure the expansion accurately enough to determine whether dark energy is a constant attribute of empty space, as Einstein proposed, or whether it shows signs of any structure, which would be consistent with modern unified theories of physics.

INDEX

A

acceleration, 92–95
Adler, Friedrich, 160
airplane, 76–77
atomic bomb, 174–184, 201
automobile, 75–76
Avogadro's number, 122–124,
    126–128

B

Bauhaus School, 54–55
Besso, Michael, 7, 64, 65
"Beyond Einstein" NASA program,
    237–239
black body radiation, 73–74
black holes, 148–149, 221–222,
    238–239
blue sky, 153–155
Bohr, Niels, 61–63, 141–142, 146, 147
Bose, Satyendra Nath, 60, 110–112,
    213–214
Braille, Louis, 204
Brown, Robert, 107–108
Brownian motion, 107–110

C

Capon, Laura, 60
compass, 90–92, 202–204
cosmological constant, 104–107,
    222–224, 238
cosmology, 95–98
critical opalescence, 153–155
Curie, Marie Sklodowska, 68–70, 111
Curie, Pierre, 69

D

Darwin, Charles, 43–45
de Broglie, Louis, 70–71
de Sitter, Willem, 98, 105, 106
Dirac, Paul Adrien, 60
Doppler, Christian, 80
Dukas, Helen, 23, 29
dyslexia, 7–9, 50

E

Edison, Thomas Alva, 47–49, 204
Eidgenössische Technische Hochschule
    (ETH), 4, 8, 10, 19–20, 64, 160,
    190–191